EASTERN SHORE LEAGUE

mike Lambert
2023

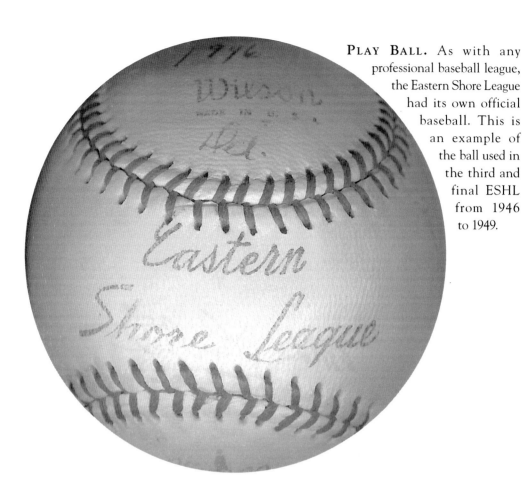

PLAY BALL. As with any professional baseball league, the Eastern Shore League had its own official baseball. This is an example of the ball used in the third and final ESHL from 1946 to 1949.

FRONT COVER: Baseball Hall of Famer and Eastern Shore native Frank "Home Run" Baker played for and managed the Easton Farmers in the Eastern Shore League during the 1924 season. (Courtesy of Brace Photo.)

COVER BACKGROUND: Pictured is the 1937 Salisbury Indians team; led by manager Jake Flowers, this squad is ranked eighth out of the top 100 minor-league teams of all time.

BACK COVER: Taken at the Milford ballpark, this is a team photograph of the 1948 Federalsburg A's. (Courtesy of Ducky Detweiler.)

EASTERN SHORE LEAGUE

Mike Lambert

ARCADIA
PUBLISHING

Published by Arcadia Publishing
Charleston, South Carolina

Printed in the United States of America

Library of Congress Control Number: 2009936120

For all general information contact Arcadia Publishing at:
Telephone 843-853-2070
Fax 843-853-0044
E-mail sales@arcadiapublishing.com
For customer service and orders:
Toll-Free 1-888-313-2665

Visit us on the Internet at www.arcadiapublishing.com

*This book is dedicated to Jennings Leroy Muir;
I will carry your friendship with me forever.*

CONTENTS

ACKNOWLEDGMENTS

I would like to express my gratitude to many individuals for their wonderful friendship and support for this project. Thank you to the Milford Museum in Delaware and Bob Voshell for his enthusiasm and faith in this project. I also want to express my appreciation to Ben Peterson, Mary Brace (Bracephoto.com), Clifford Collison, William Hill, Ann Adams, and Robert "Ducky" and Jean Detweiler for their contributions to this book. Thank you to my wife, Cara, who supports me in everything I do; and last but not least, I must give a very special thank you to Donnie Davidson from Cambridge, Maryland. Without Donnie's remarkable collection and endless knowledge of the Eastern Shore League, this book would not have been possible. Unless otherwise noted, all images are from the collections of Mr. Davidson and myself.

INTRODUCTION

The purpose of writing this book is to help keep the history of the Eastern Shore League (ESHL) alive for future generations. Using many previously unpublished photographs and one-of-a-kind artifacts from private collections to tell the league's story, this book allows readers a unique opportunity to see and feel these three wonderful eras of professional baseball on the Delmarva Peninsula. Although not intended to be a comprehensive history of the three ESHLs, this book offers fans a chance to escape back to the glory days of professional baseball on the Eastern Shore.

For more than 100 years, baseball has been a constant on Delmarva. Town ball, semi-professional, and professional minor leagues have all graced the Eastern Shore's many baseball diamonds, but it is the rich history of the three-term professional class-D Eastern Shore League that is most compelling for any local fan of minor-league baseball history. From Dover, Delaware, to Parksley, Virginia, to Cambridge, Maryland, from the 1920s through the 1940s, baseball was the social event to attend. Bearing team names such as the Spuds, Canners, Farmers, Yankees, Orioles, and Crabbers, clubs filled the stands with fans who cheered passionately for their heroes, many of whom hailed from right here on the Eastern Shore.

During the first Eastern Shore League (1922–1928), fans could watch future Hall of Famers Home Run Baker, Jimmie Foxx, Red Ruffing, and Mickey Cochrane ply their trade as well as future Baltimore Orioles manager Paul Richards.

The second Eastern Shore League opened in 1937 and ended after the 1941 season. Its star players included Mel Parnell, Carl Furillo, Ducky Detweiler, Danny Murtaugh, and Mickey Vernon. During this era, many future major-leaguers honed their skills around the Eastern Shore. Most of the team names mimicked the names of their major-league affiliates, like the Yankees, Red Sox, Giants, Cardinals, A's, Indians, and Orioles, although there were a few exceptions (the Colts and Chicks, for instance.) During their remarkable 1937 season, the Salisbury Indians won the league championship despite having to forfeit 21 victories. They are still considered one of the top 10 minor-league teams of all time.

The third and final ESHL began in 1946 and ceased operations after the conclusion of the 1949 season. My own hometown of Seaford, Delaware, won the 1947 league championship, beating the Cambridge Dodgers in a seven-game playoff. Notable players from this last installment of the ESHL included Duke Markell, Steve Bilko, Chris Van Cuyk, Joe Muir, Ray Jablonski, Norm Zauchin, Don Zimmer, Gene Corbett, and Bill Ripken—uncle of Hall of Famer Cal Ripken Jr.

Having collected and studied this glorious baseball league for several decades, I am committed to teaching its history at every opportunity. I hope you'll take the time to view the rare original tickets, programs, contracts, stock certificates, balls, bats, letters, schedules, and photographs that grace the pages of this book. By reading the story behind these extraordinary artifacts and studying the interesting facts of the ESHL, you will not only learn about the Eastern Shore League, but you will also understand how minor-league baseball operated from the 1920s through the 1940s.

1922 PARKSLEY SPUDS. Managed by Thomas "Poke" Whalen, this Parksley team would go down in history as the first Eastern Shore League pennant winner, with 42 wins and 25 losses. Pitcher William Klingelhoefer led the team with 15 wins (with just 5 losses). The Spuds won three pennants in the league's six-year existence, earning the team dynasty status in the 1920s.

BALL ONE
1922–1928

By the start of the 1920s, the Eastern Shore had enjoyed semi-professional baseball for many years. However, the citizens of Delmarva were very excited to have professional baseball arrive in the spring of 1922. The original class-D ESHL at various times included teams from three states: Delaware (Dover and Laurel), Maryland (Crisfield, Cambridge, Salisbury, Easton, and Pocomoke City), and Virginia (Parksley and Northampton). In 1923, Milford, Delaware, fielded a team that quit the league in July rather than abide by the league rule that permitted only three class players (players with more than 25 games of experience at a higher level) per team.

The Parksley Spuds were ESHL champions three times during the 1922–1928 era, including the league's first and final full years, 1922 and 1927. Although short-lived, this first ESHL provided local baseball fans with many memories during those six seasons, including the opportunity to witness the beginning of Jimmie Foxx's magnificent career under the tutelage of the aging Frank "Home Run" Baker in Easton. Both of these future Hall of Famers were Maryland Eastern Shore natives, Baker from Trappe and Foxx from Sudlersville.

The league's Delaware fans were treated to two future Hall of Famers themselves, with Mickey Cochrane and Red Ruffing both playing for Dover (Cochrane in 1923 and Ruffing in 1924). Many other players from the first ESHL made it to the big leagues as well, including future Orioles and White Sox manager Paul Richards and Cambridge native Jake Flowers.

The ESHL began a 1928 season, but after many attempts to bolster the wavering attendance, league directors voted to disband on July 11, annulling all 1928 statistics-to-date and formally ending the league's initial run after six seasons. The Eastern Shore League dissolved and would disappear from the Delmarva Peninsula for 10 long years.

1922 CAMBRIDGE CANNERS. Managed by Herb Armstrong and sparked by future major-league Jake Flowers, the Cambridge, Maryland, club finished the 1922 season in second place. The 20-year-old Flowers hit for a .312 average and led the league with 14 home runs. Workhorse pitcher Edward Schroll led the league in innings pitched with 205.

1922 Schedule For   *Cambridge Baseball*

AT HOME with			ABROAD with		
Salisbury............June 13 24			*Salisbury*............June 12 23		
July 8 18 31			July 5 17		
Aug. 12			Aug. 1 11		
Sep. 4 a. m.			Sep. 4, p. m.		
Crisfield............June 15 27			*Crisfield*............June 14 26		
July 7 20			July 8 19		
Aug. 6 16 25			Aug. 3 (15) 26		
Pocomoke............June 19 30			*Pocomoke*............June 20		
July 12 26			July 1 13 27		
Aug. 8 19			Aug. 7 22		
Sep. 1			Sep. 2		
Parksley ....June 13 29			*Parksley* ....June 16 28		
July 11 22			July 10 21		
Aug. 18 31			Aug. 5 17 30		
Laurel ....June 9 21			*Laurel*............June 10 22		
July a.m. 14 29			July 4 p.m. 15 28		
Aug. 9 23			Aug. 10 24		

1922 CAMBRIDGE CANNERS SCHEDULE. This Cambridge schedule shows that Delaware and Virginia each had only one league entry for the 1922 season: Laurel and Parksley, respectively. All of the other teams were from Maryland.

BALL ONE: 1922–1928

1923 MILFORD SANDPIPERS SCHEDULE. This extremely rare schedule for the 1923 Milford Sandpipers includes many games that were never played. The Sandpipers dropped out of the league in early July after refusing to obey the league rule of fielding no more than three class players—a player who had played 25 games or more in a higher division. This violation meant that Milford would have to forfeit all of the team's victories, and the Milford team decided to quit rather than forfeit its wins. (Courtesy of Bob Voshell.)

Schedule of Games

OF

Milford Base Ball Club

SEASON OF 1923

Milford At Home	Milford Away From Home
May 26—Dover at Milford	May 25—Milford at Dover
May 29—Salisbury at Milford	May 28—Milford at Salisbury
May 31—Cambridge at Milford	May 30—Milford at Cambridge.
June 2—Pocomoke at Milford	June 1—Milford at Pocomoke
June 5—Parksley at Milford	June 4—Milford at Parksley
June 6—Laurel at Milford	June 7—Milford at Laurel
June 8—Crisfield at Milford	June 9—Milford at Crisfield
June 11—Dover at Milford	June 12—Milford at Dover
June 13—Salisbury at Milford	June 14—Milford at Salisbury
June 15—Cambridge at Milford	June 16—Milford at Cambridge
June 20—Parksley at Milford	June 18—Milford at Parksley
June 21—Pocomoke at Milford	June 19—Milford at Pocomoke
June 23—Laurel at Milford	June 22—Milford at Laurel
June 26—Crisfield at Milford	June 25—Milford at Crisfield
June 28—Cambridge at Milford	June 27—Milford at Cambridge
June 30—Salisbury at Milford	June 29—Milford at Salisbury
July 4—Dover at Milford (afternoon)	July 4—Milford at Dover (morning)
July 5—Pocomoke at Milford	July 6—Milford at Pocomoke
July 7—Parksley at Milford	July 10—Milford at Parksley
July 12—Laurel at Milford	July 11—Milford at Laurel
July 14—Crisfield at Milford	July 13—Milford at Crisfield
July 16—Cambridge at Milford	July 17—Milford at Cambridge
July 18—Salisbury at Milford	July 19—Milford at Salisbury
July 20—Dover at Milford	July 21—Milford at Dover
July 23—Pocomoke at Milford	July 25—Milford at Pocomoke
July 24—Parksley at Milford	July 26—Milford at Parksley
July 27—Laurel at Milford	July 28—Milford at Laurel
July 31—Crisfield at Milford	July 30—Milford at Crisfield
Aug. 1—Cambridge at Milford	Aug. 2—Milford at Cambride
Aug. 3—Salisbury at Milford	Aug. 4—Milford at Salisbury
Aug. 6—Dover at Milford	Aug. 7—Milford at Dover
Aug. 9—Parksley at Milford	Aug. 8—Milford at Pocomoke
Aug. 10—Pocomoke at Milford	Aug. 11—Milford at Parksley
Aug. 14—Laurel at Milford	Aug. 15—Milford at Laurel
Aug. 16—Crisfield at Milford	Aug. 17—Milford at Crisfield
Aug. 18—Dover at Milford	Aug. 21—Milford at Dover
Aug. 23—Cambridge at Milford	Aug. 22—Milford at Cambridge
Aug. 25—Salisbury at Milford	Aug. 24—Milford at Salisbury
Aug. 27—Parksley at Milford	Aug. 28—Milford at Parksley
Aug. 30—Pocomoke at Milford	Aug. 29—Milford at Pocomoke
Aug. 31—Crisfield at Milford	Sept. 1—Milford at Crisfield
Sept. 3—Laurel at Milford (afternoon)	Sept. 3—Milford at Laurel (morning)

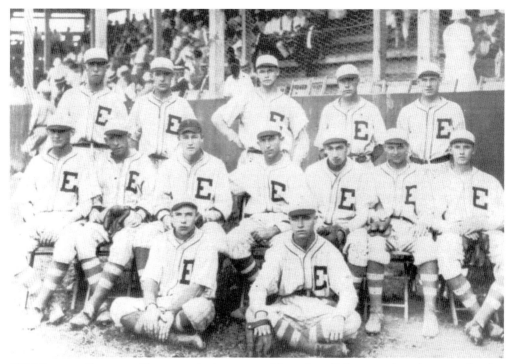

1924 EASTON FARMERS. Former major-league star Home Run Baker was player/manager for this team, which was also the first professional team for Baker's fellow Eastern Shore native, Jimmie Foxx. Though the 1924 Farmers finished in last place, Easton fans that year cheered on two future Hall of Fame players in the 16-year-old Foxx and the 38-year-old Baker. In this photograph, Baker sits in the center and Foxx stands directly behind him.

Know all Men by These Presents:

THAT I, _Easton Coca Cola Bottling Co._

do hereby constitute and appoint _Jas. C. Godwin_

of Talbot County, State of Maryland, as my lawful proxy, for me and in my name, place and stead, to vote all the shares of the Capital Stock of The Easton Baseball Club of Talbot County, Inc., standing in my name on Books of the Company, at all meetings of the shareholders thereof, annual, adjourned or special, for the election of Directors and for such other purposes as require the action of the shareholders. This proxy shall conitnue in force for a period of _One_ years, unless sooner revoked.

In Witness Whereof, I have hereunto set my hand and seal this _eleventh_

day of _October_ Nineteen Hundred and _Twenty Four_

Sealed and Delivered, in the Presence of

J. L. Godwin _Easton Coca Cola Bottling Co._ (SEAL)

Caroll C. Ham, Mgr.

1924 EASTON FARMERS STOCK PROXY. This particularly rare stock proxy for the Easton Baseball Club, signed October 11, 1924, allows the appointed person to vote for the shareholder at all meetings.

EASTERN SHORE BASEBALL SCHEDULE
Season 1924

For	AT PARKSLEY	AT SALISBURY	AT CRISFIELD	AT DOVER	AT EASTON	AT CAMBRIDGE
rksley....	**Best**	May 30 June 11, 25 July 5, 16, 28 Aug. 8, 21	June 2, 13, 26 July 4A., 19,30 Aug. 11 Sept. 1 P. M.	June 7, 19 July 1, 11, 24 Aug. 5, 15, 27	June 9, 20 July 2, 12, 25 Aug. 6, 19, 30	June 4, 17, ? July 8 ? Aug. 1, 11, ?
lisbury...	May 31 June 12,23 July 7, 17, 29 Aug. 9, 22	**Sports**	June 10, 21 July 2, 15, 25 Aug. 6, 20, 29	June 2, 13, 26 July 4A., 19, 31 Aug. 11 Sept. 1 A. M.	June 4, 17, 28 July 8, 22 Aug. 2, 13, 23	June 6, 19, 30 July 19, 23 Aug. 5, 15, 27
isfield....	June 3,14, 25 July 4P., 18,31 Aug. 12 Sept. 1, A. M.	June 9, 20 July 3, 12, 26 Aug. 7, 19, 30	**Read**	June 4, 16, 28 July 8, 21 Aug. 1, 13, 26	June 6, 18, 30 July 10, 24 Aug. 5, 15, 28	May 30 June 11, 24 July 5, 16, 29 Aug. ? ?
ver........	June 6, 18,30 July 10, 23 Aug. 4, 16, 28 June 10, 21	June 3, 14, 25 July 4A., 18, 30 Aug. 12 Sept. 1 P. M.	June 5, 17, 27 July 9, 22 Aug. 2, 14, 23	**The**	May 31 June 11, 23 July 5, 16, 28 Aug. 8, 22	June 9, 20 July 2, 12, 25 Aug. 7, 20, 29
ston......	June 10,21 July 3, 15, 26 Aug. 7, 20, 29	June 5, 16, 27 July 9, 21 Aug. 1, 14, 26	June 7, 19 July 1, 11, 23 Aug. 4, 16, 27	May 30 June 12, 24 July 7, 17, 29 Aug. 9, 21	**Baltimore**	June 2, 14, 26 July ?, 19, 31 Aug. 12 Sept. 1 P. M.
nbridge.	July 3, 15, 26 Aug. 7, 20, 29 June 5, 16, 27 July 9, 22 Aug. 2, 13, 26	June 7, 18 July 1, 11, 24 Aug. 4, 16, 28	May 31 June 12, 23 July 7, 17, 28 Aug. 8, 22	June 10, 21 July 3, 15, 26 Aug. 6, 19, 30	June 3, 13, 25 July 4P., 18, 30 Aug. 11 Sept. 1 A. M.	**News!**

1924 EASTERN SHORE LEAGUE SCHEDULE. The 1924 season was the first for the Easton Farmers, and Dover was left as the only Delaware entry in the ESHL—the Laurel Blue Hens had dropped out after the 1923 season. The schedule here doubles as an advertising piece for a Baltimore, Maryland, newspaper. In 1924, the Parksley Spuds won the pennant for the second time in three years with a 46-34 record.

PAUL RICHARDS. Shown here in a Brooklyn Dodgers uniform is Paul Richards, who played in 1926 and 1927 for the Crisfield Crabbers. A baseball man for life, Richards later played, managed, and served as a general manager in the major leagues. The several highlights in Richards's career include catching all seven games of the 1945 World Series for the world champion Detroit Tigers and once pitching in a minor-league game using both his arms, alternating them from pitch to pitch.

1928 CRISFIELD CRABBERS LETTER. The last sentence of this letter from the Crabbers' treasurer, W. E. Riggin, illustrates how attendance (or lack of same) was on the minds of ESHL front officers in 1928. The league would collapse six days after this letter was written.

Crisfield, Md.
July 5, 1928.

Mr. Robert H. Matthews, Tres.
    Cambridge, Md.

Dear Sir:-

        I herewith inclose check of $377.60 for 944 paid addmissions for Baseball game played in Crisfield, Md.afternoon of July 4th, 1928,between Salisbury and Crisfield.

                Also wish to send you a list of attendance up until this time.

June				admissions	
6	- Easton at Crisfield			384 admissions.	15.36
7	- Northampton at	"		208	8.32
9	- Cambridge	"	"	355	14.20
12	- Parksley	"	"	225	9.00
15 *	Salisbury	"	"	449	17.96
18	- Easton	"	"	361	14.44
19	- Northampton	"	"	316	12.64
21	- Cambridge	"	"	301	12.04
23	- Parksley	"	"	530	21.20
26	- Easton	"	"	251	10.04
28	- Northampton	"	"	286	11.44
30	- Cambridge	"	"	305	12.20
	Total-			3973	

Hoping we will enjoy better attendance in the future, I am,

                Yours respectfully,

                    W. E. Riggin, Treasurer.

J. HARRY REW,
PRESIDENT
WALTER B. MILLER,
VICE-PRESIDENT
M. B. THAWLEY,
VICE-PRESIDENT
ROBERT H. MATTHEWS,
TREASURER
JAMES A. McALLISTER,
SECRETARY

CAMBRIDGE, MD.
CRISFIELD, MD.
EASTON, MD.
SALISBURY, MD.
DOVER, DEL.
PARKSLEY, VA.

THE EASTERN SHORE LEAGUE

OF PROFESSIONAL BASE BALL CLUBS

—— FROM THE ——

OFFICE OF THE SECRETARY

CAMBRIDGE, MARYLAND

December 5th, 1925.

Mr. Robert H. Matthews,
Treasurer, Eastern Shore League,
Cambridge, Maryland.

Dear Sir;-

Your report for the 1925 season was read at the annual Fall meeting of this league, at Salisbury, yesterday, and highly complimented.

At this meeting, the salary of the league statistician for the past season was fixed at $150.00.

Also, the Parksley club was allowed the sum of $100.00, to be paid from the league treasury, for money withheld by the Easton club for rental of the Easton park for the 1924 post season series game with Martinsburg.

Mr. Whealton, of Salisbury, stated that neither Easton nor Crisfield have settled with Salisbury, as he advised you, while Mr. Tawes, of Crisfield, stated that he has never been able to obtain a record of the official attendance at the last game of Crisfield at Easton, besides never having been paid for this game. I advised both Mr. Whealton and Mr. Tawes that you have no funds in hand belonging to Easton. Crisfield and Salisbury evidently are ready to agree on their debt.

Very truly yours,

James A. McAllister,
Secretary.

1925 EASTERN SHORE LEAGUE LETTER. This letter between league secretary James McAllister and treasurer Robert Matthews offers another look at the delicate role that finances played during the ESHL's entire existence. Note that the league's statistician was paid just $150 for the entire season.

EASTERN SHORE LEAGUE BASEBALL PARK, PARKSLEY, VA.

PARKSLEY SPUDS BALLPARK. The postcard above features a nice view of the Parksley, Virginia, stadium where the Spuds saw action for six seasons in the 1920s, winning the pennant three times.

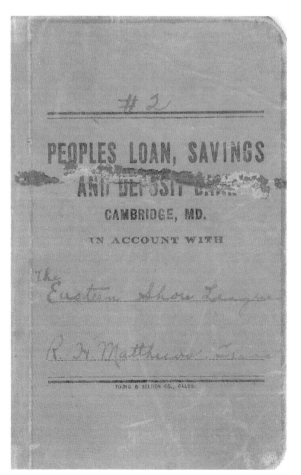

1927 EASTERN SHORE LEAGUE BANK BOOK. During the 1927 season, league treasurer Robert Matthews recorded the bank balance for the ESHL in this book. The league's bank was Peoples Loan and Deposit Bank in Cambridge, Maryland.

1923 CAMBRIDGE CANNERS STOCK CERTIFICATE. Above is a Cambridge Maryland Athletic Association stock certificate for one $10 share sold to league treasurer Robert Matthews in February 1923.

1923 MILFORD TICKET STUB. The Sandpipers of Milford, Delaware, folded soon after the 1923 season had begun. Now exceptionally rare, this ticket from the Milford Base Ball Club originally sold for 20¢.

EASTERN SHORE LEAGUE, 1925

Baltimore	AT CAMBRIDGE.	AT CRISFIELD.	AT DOVER.	AT EASTON.	AT PARKSLEY.	AT SALISBURY
CAMBRIDGE ..	Sun	May 28 July 3, 13 July 2, 13 July 24 Aug. 6, 18 Aug. 29	June 5, 15 July 1, 11 July 23 Aug. 4, 14 Aug. 27 Sept. 5	May 30 June 11, 22 July 4, P. M. July 15, 28 Aug. 8, 20 Sept. 7, A. M.	June 1, 12 June 24 July 7, 18 July 30 Aug. 10, 21 Aug. 31	June 3 June 17, 27 July 9, 21 July 31 Aug. 12 Aug. 24 Sept. 2
CRISFIELD	May 27 June 5, 19 July 25 Aug. 5, 17 Aug. 28	Gives	June 1, 13 June 25 July 6, 18 July 29 Aug. 10, 21 Sept. 1	June 3, 18 June 27 July 8, 21 July 31 Aug. 12, 24 Sept. 3	May 30 June 10, 23 July 4, A. M. July 16, 28 Aug. 7, 20 Sept. 7, A. M.	June 5, 16 June 30 July 11, 23 Aug. 3, 14 Aug. 26 Sept. 5
DOVER	June 6, 16 June 30 July 10, 22 Aug. 15 Aug. 26 Sept. 4	June 2, 12 June 24 July 7, 17 July 30 Aug. 11, 22 Aug. 31	This	May 28 June 9, 20 July 2, 13 July 25 Aug. 5, 18 Aug. 28	June 3, 18 June 27 July 8, 20 July 31 Aug. 12, 24 Sept. 3	May 30 June 11, 22 July 4, P. M. July 15, 28 Aug. 7, 20 Sept. 7, A. M.
EASTON	May 29 June 10, 23, M. July 4, M. July 16, 27 Aug. 7, P. M. Sept. 7, P. M.	June 4, 17 June 26 July 9, 20 Aug. 1, 13 Aug. 25 Sept. 2	May 27 June 8, 19 July 3, 14 July 24 Aug. 6, 17 Aug. 29	League's	June 6, 15 July 1, 11 July 23 Aug. 4, 15 Aug. 27 Sept. 4	June 1, 13 June 25 July 7, 17 July 30 Aug. 11, 22 Aug. 31
PARKSLEY	June 2, 13 June 25 July 6 July 29 Aug. 11, 22 Sept. 1	May 29 June 11, 22 July 4 P. M. July 15, 27 Aug. 8, 19 Sept. 7 P. M.	June 4, 17 June 26 July 9, 21 Aug. 1, 13 Aug. 25 Sept. 2	June 5, 16 June 30 July 10, 22 Aug. 3, 14 Aug. 26 Sept. 5	Box	May 27 June 9, 19 July 2, 13 July 25 Aug. 5, 17 Aug. 28
SALISBURY	June 4, 18 June 26 July 8, 20 Aug. 1, 13 Aug. 25 Sept. 3	June 6, 15 July 1, 10 July 22 Aug. 4, 15 Aug. 27 Sept. 4	May 29 June 10, 23 July 4 A. M. July 16, 27 Aug. 8, 19 Sept. 7 P. M.	June 2, 12 June 24 July 6, 18 July 29 Aug. 10, 21 Sept. 1	May 28 June 8, 20 July 6, 14 July 24 Aug. 6, 18 Aug. 29	Scores

The Baltimore Sun's Sports Pages Always Interest the Baseball Fan

1925 EASTERN SHORE LEAGUE SCHEDULE. The Baltimore *Sun* newspaper issued this schedule for the entire 1925 ESHL season. Led by pitcher John Trippe, the Cambridge Canners won the pennant that year. Trippe went 18-5 for a league-leading .783 winning percentage. Parksley's John Firth led the league with 21 victories.

HOME RUN BAKER. Pictured above in his Philadelphia Athletics uniform, Baker played and managed at Easton in the 1924 ESHL after a stellar major-league career that ultimately earned him a place in the Baseball Hall of Fame. (Courtesy of Brace Photo.)

THE EASTERN SHORE LEAGUE
Professional Base Ball Clubs
J. HARRY REW, President

Cambridge, Md.
Crisfield, Md.
Easton, Md.

Cape Charles, Va.
Salisbury, Md.
Parksley, Va.

Parksley, Virginia

June 12th, 1928.

Mr. Robert H. Matthews,
Treasurer E. S. League,
Cambridge, Md.
Dear Mr. Matthews:-

I think it best that you retain $50.00
from McTague's check on the first pay day and let me have
check for that amount so that I can pay his fine. I hope
you will carefully scrutinize the expense accounts and keep
them down as much as possible. McTague and Morgan, I understand, are using their own automobiles and we should settle
with them, I think, on the same basis as with Guyon last year.
In the case of Butler I particularly told him that he must
ride in the club busses whenever possible and we would not
allow transportation expenses when the bus could have been
used. As I told you I do not think we should allow any
expenses except transportation charges.

Thanking you and with best wishes, I am

Yours very truly,
J. Harry Rew

P. S. What do you think of Butler as an Umpire?

1928 EASTERN SHORE LEAGUE LETTER. Written by league president J. Harry Rew shortly before the league folded, this June 12, 1928, letter expresses Rew's desire to cut the league's costs. He urges ESHL treasurer Robert Matthews to "carefully scrutinize the expense accounts," and declares that if umpire H. J. Butler chooses to drive his own car to the ballpark rather than riding a team bus, he will not be reimbursed for his transportation costs.

EASTERN SHORE'S FINEST AND MOST MODERN HOTEL
HOSPITALITY AND GOOD CHEER

ABSOLUTELY FIREPROOF

EUROPEAN PLAN

FRED. P. ADKINS
PRESIDENT

O. G. CLEMENTS
MANAGER

WICOMICO HOTEL
150 ROOMS
SALISBURY, MD.

MANAGER'S OFFICE

July 11th, 1928

Mr. Robert H. Matthews,
Cambridge, Maryland.

My dear Mr. Matthews:-

Confirming our telephone conversation of
even date relative to the unpaid check of H.J.Butler, in
accordance with your suggestion, I beg to enclose here-with
the check in question and will appreciate it if you will
deduct this amount from what is due him by the Eastern Shore
League and send us your check for a like amount.

I very much appreciate your kindness to
me in this instance and sincerely hope that I may have the
pleasure of reciprocating same in the very near future.

Very truly yours,
THE WICOMICO HOTEL,

Manager

1928 LETTER TO LEAGUE TREASURER. In this July 11, 1928, letter to the league treasurer Robert Matthews, the manager of the Wicomico Hotel in Salisbury, Maryland, asks for assistance for an unpaid debt by league umpire H. J. Butler.

GEORGE SELKIRK. The man who replaced Babe Ruth in right field for the New York Yankees in 1935, Selkirk played for the 1927 Cambridge Canners, hitting a robust .348. In the majors, Selkirk was a two-time All-Star and a member of five New York Yankees World Series championship teams. After his playing career, Selkirk was a general manager of the Washington Senators and later scouted for the Yankees. He is a member of the Canadian Baseball Hall of Fame.

1928 SALISBURY INDIANS CHECK. Payable to league treasurer Robert Matthews, this check from the Salisbury baseball club is dated July 5, 1928. Cancelled checks from the first era of the ESHL are not easy to come by.

1928 PRINTING RECEIPT. With this June 1928 receipt, the type shop at the *Cambridge Record* requests payment for the printing of the ESHL's own receipt blanks.

HOME RUN BAKER. In this photograph taken later in life, Home Run Baker poses in street clothes. Note the tie clip with the Philadelphia Athletics logo on it.

CRISFIELD CRABBERS TICKET. This unused ESHL ticket, issued by the Crisfield Baseball Association for a bleacher seat at a Crabbers game, originally sold for a mere 30¢.

MICKEY COCHRANE AND JIMMIE FOXX. This unique photograph has former ESHL stars Mickey Cochrane and Jimmy Foxx flanking Ralph "Cy" Perkins while all three were members of the Philadelphia A's. The uniqueness of this photograph is that Foxx is shown here as a catcher. Cochrane caught for the Eastern Shore League's Dover Senators in 1923, and Foxx took up catching while playing for manager Home Run Baker in 1924 on the Easton Farmers. If great catchers such as Cochrane and Perkins hadn't also been playing for the A's, Foxx might have reached the big leagues as a catcher. Instead, he changed positions and became one of the greatest first basemen of all time.

Eastern Shore League

Games Scheduled For

DOVER

At Home
And Away

Season of 1924

Admission Price At The
Dover Park

Grandstand -   -   60c
Bleachers   -   -   40c

1924 DOVER SENATORS SCHEDULE.
For 40¢ fans could cheer on the Dover
Senators during the 1924 season. At left
is the schedule for the ESHL team in
Dover, Delaware. Future Hall of Famer
Charles "Red" Ruffing started 1924 with
Dover and ended the year in the major
leagues, pitching for the Boston Red Sox.

FARMERS TICKET. Below is a
ticket stub from the Easton
Baseball Club in the 1920s.

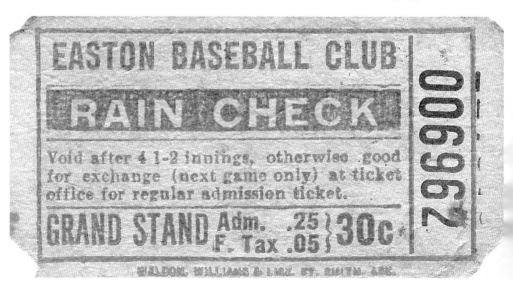

EASTON BASEBALL CLUB

RAIN CHECK

Void after 4 1-2 innings, otherwise good
for exchange (next game only) at ticket
office for regular admission ticket.

GRAND STAND Adm. .25 } 30c
F. Tax .05 }

296900

WELDON, WILLIAMS & LICK, FT. SMITH, ARK.

JAKE FLOWERS MAJOR-LEAGUE BAT. Eastern Shore native D'Arcy Jake Flowers used this bat during his baseball career. Flowers played for Cambridge in 1922 and 1923 and went on to play for several teams in the major leagues, including the Brooklyn Dodgers. Flowers later managed in the second ESHL at Salisbury and Pocomoke City.

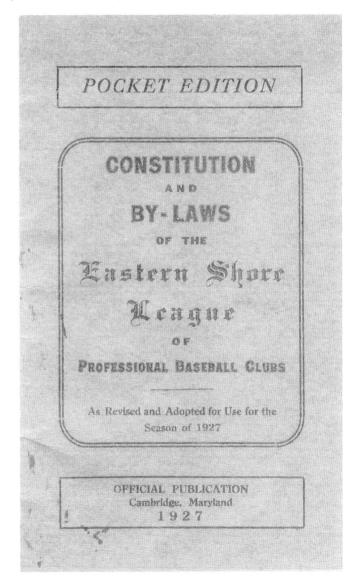

EASTERN SHORE LEAGUE BYLAWS. At right, this 1927 pocket version of the ESHL's constitution and bylaws provides an insightful look at the rules used during that period.

EASTERN SHORE LEAGUE CHECK. Based in Cambridge, Maryland, the Peoples Loan, Savings, and Deposit Bank was the ESHL's bank of choice during the 1920s. This is an unused check from that era.

1927 EASTERN SHORE LEAGUE RECEIPT. This 1927 receipt form was typically used when the league received its 10-percent share of the ticket sales for each game played by its teams.

1922 CAMBRIDGE BALLPARK. Taken during the 1922 season at the ballpark in Cambridge, Maryland, this image shows notable men from the ESHL and several other leagues. The men pictured here are, from left to right, (kneeling) John Noble, unidentified, L. D. T. Noble, Emmett Ewell, Frederick Stevens, Sidney Henry, unidentified, Daniel Wright, and Frank Robbins; (standing) W. Carl Bradley, Robert H. Matthews Sr., Calvin Harrington Sr., American League president Ban Johnson, Samuel W. Lithicum, former Maryland governor Emerson C. Harrington, Judge Josiah Bayley, P. Watson Webb, unidentified, Harry Rue, Dr. Brice W. Goldsborough, and Blue Ridge League president J. Vincent Jamison. Visible in the grandstands are Charles and Carroll Dill, Duncan Noble, Mrs. Noble, and Jean Noble Chaffinch. Johnson was instrumental in founding and popularizing the American League and is a charter member of the Baseball Hall of Fame.

JIMMIE FOXX. Eastern Shore native Jimmie Foxx began his professional baseball career in 1924 playing in the ESHL. Foxx was a star for many years with the Philadelphia A's and the Boston Red Sox. He also played for the Chicago Cubs and the Philadelphia Phillies and ultimately earned a place in Cooperstown.

1929 JIMMIE FOXX BASKETBALL TICKET. Shown below is a rare ticket to a basketball contest in Seaford, a game played by Jimmie Foxx's All-Stars and the Seaford Athletic Club's basketball team during the winter of 1929.

BASKET BALL

SEAFORD "SACS"

vs.

JIMMY FOXX'S "ALL STARS"

FRIDAY, FEBRUARY 15, 1929

8.00 P. M.

ADMISSION 50 CENTS

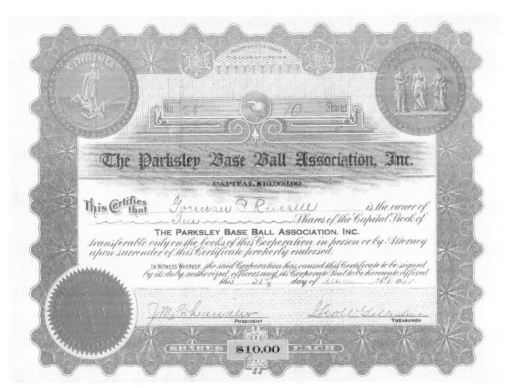

1922 PARKSLEY STOCK CERTIFICATE.
Shown above is Parksley Base Ball
Association, Inc., Stock Certificate No.
54, issued in May 1922 for 10 shares at $10
each. Records suggest that less than 100 of
these stock certificates were ever issued.

1928 UMPIRE EXPENSE REPORT. Umpire H. J.
Butler recorded his travel costs on stationary
from the Delmarva Hotel in Cape Charles,
Virginia. Butler's expenses are for trips
between Cape Charles and Parksley and from
Easton to Cape Charles. This unique item is
from early in the never-completed 1928 season.

Base Ball Recorder

FOLLOW THE GAMES
DOVER AT HOME

July 1, 11, 24 . . . . Parksley
July 3, 15, 26 . . . . Cambridge
July 4—P. M.—19, 31 . . . . Salisbury
July 7, 17, 29 . . . . Easton
July 8, 21 . . . . Crisfield
Aug. 1, 13, 26 . . . . Crisfield
Aug. 5, 15, 27 . . . . Parksley
Aug. 6, 19, 30 . . . . Cambridge
Aug. 9, 21 . . . . Easton
Aug. 11 . . . . Salisbury
Sept. 1—A. M. . . . . Salisbury

DOVER ABROAD

July 2, 12, 25 . . . . Cambridge
July 4—A. M.—18, 30 . . . . Salisbury
July 5, 16, 28 . . . . Easton
July 9, 22 . . . . Crisfield
July 10, 23 . . . . Parksley
Aug. 2, 14, 23 . . . . Crisfield
Aug. 4, 16, 28 . . . . Parksley
Aug. 7, 20, 29 . . . . Cambridge
Aug. 8, 22 . . . . Easton
Aug. 12 . . . . Salisbury
Sept. 1—P. M. . . . . Salisbury

DOVER BASE BALL RECORDER. This rare 1920s advertising item from the Dover Senators features the team's entire schedule on the cover. On the inside is an advertisement for a local lumber and milling company and a unique device for recording a baseball score. Fans could track the game by moving the brass dials around to mark each inning, out, hit, run, and error.

Compliments of

DOVER LUMBER & MILLING CO.

So. State St.   Phone 288

Headquarters for

All Kinds of Building Material

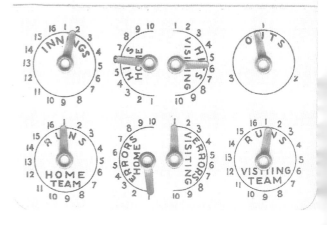

BALL TWO
1937–1941

After a 10-year absence, the Eastern Shore League returned to the Delmarva Peninsula for the 1937 season, beginning a second run that would last for five seasons. Maryland had the most entries during this era; it fielded teams from Cambridge, Centreville, Easton, Salisbury, Federalsburg, Crisfield, and Pocomoke City. The Delaware entries hailed from Dover and Milford. Virginia did not return a team to the league and never would.

Tom Kibler of Washington College was very instrumental in organizing the second ESHL. He began the 1937 season as league president and was the one who made the decision to force the Salisbury Indians to forfeit 21 wins due to their use of an illegal player. In one day, Salisbury's record went from 21-5 to 0-26. Still, manager Jake Flowers held his team together to win 48 out of their next 58 games and capture the pennant, setting a new attendance record along the way. This amazing feat did not escape the media's notice: Flowers was named the *Sporting News* Minor-League Manager of the Year, an award usually reserved for managers at a much higher level.

This second ESHL was noted for its rowdy fans and fights on the field, including a notable altercation between the managers of the Cambridge and Centreville teams. Prominent future big-leaguers from this era included Carl Furillo, Mickey Vernon, Sid Gordon, and Mel Parnell.

With the advent of World War II, even the major leagues had trouble operating and locating quality players, and minor-league clubs had a much harder time. Consequently, having suffered from low attendance even in peacetime, the Eastern Shore League shut down after the 1941 season, ending professional baseball on Delmarva once again.

EASTERN SHORE LEAGUE UMPIRES. This 1940 photograph portrays two unidentified umpires.

JOCKO THOMPSON. A pitcher for the Centreville Red Sox in 1940, Thompson finished the season 18-5, with an extraordinary 1.56 ERA. He went on to play for the Philadelphia Phillies from 1948 to 1951.

1937 SALISBURY INDIANS. Considered one of minor-league baseball's best teams ever, the 1937 Salisbury, Maryland, team won the pennant even after having to forfeit 21 victories for using an illegal player. The *Sporting News* named Jake Flowers Minor-League Manager of the Year, and players Joe Kohlman, Jorge Comellas, Mike Guerra, Frank Trechock, Ed Leip, and Jerry Lynn were all later promoted to the Washington Senators. From left to right, the team and its staff pictured here are (first row) batboy Morris Fields, Bill Luzansky, Joe Reznichak, Mike Guerra, Charles Quimby, Jerry Lynn, and Edgar Leip; (second row) team treasurer John Milton, Fred Thomas, manager Jake Flowers, John Bassler, Leon Revolinsky, Joe Garliss, Joe Kohlman, and business manager Melvin Murphy; (third row) Jorge Comellas, Juan Montero, Frank Trechock, and Frank Deutsch.

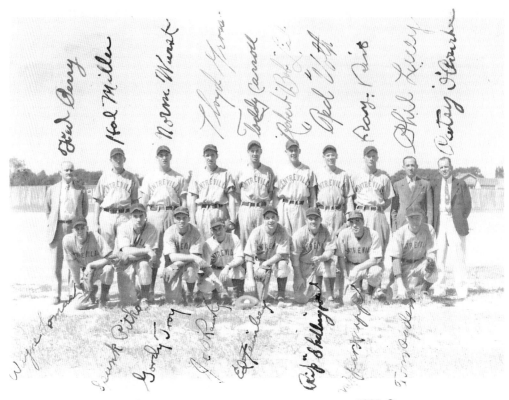

1937 CENTREVILLE COLTS. The Boston Red Sox affiliate team from Centreville, Maryland, was led by Alex Pitko and Ed Feinberg, who in an 84-game season produced 35 home runs and 142 RBI between them. Pitchers Tom Ogden and Lloyd Gross led the team in wins with 14 and 13 respectively. The photograph at left shows some of the Colts players before a game.

1937 Salisbury Indians Collage. This collage made by a fan commemorates the Salisbury Indians' winning the league championship in 1937. Note the headline referring to Joe Kohlman's no-hitter, which clinched the Indians' championship.

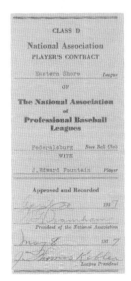

1937 Player Contract. Signed by ESHL president Tom Kibler and dated May 1937, this official league document contracts J. Edward Fountain to play for the Federalsburg A's.

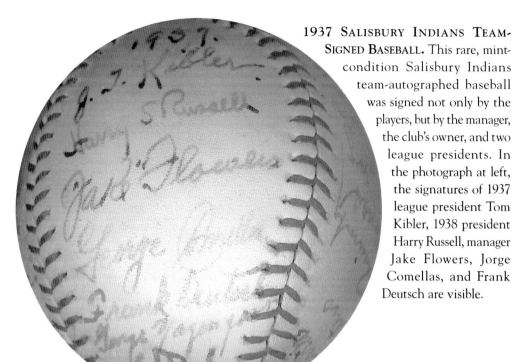

1937 Salisbury Indians Team-Signed Baseball. This rare, mint-condition Salisbury Indians team-autographed baseball was signed not only by the players, but by the manager, the club's owner, and two league presidents. In the photograph at left, the signatures of 1937 league president Tom Kibler, 1938 president Harry Russell, manager Jake Flowers, Jorge Comellas, and Frank Deutsch are visible.

1937 Salisbury Indians Team-Signed Baseball, Second View. This image shows the signatures of Indians owner Joe Cambria, Juan Montero, Charles Quimby, Fred Thomas, Leon Revolinsky, and Joe Garliss.

BALL TWO: 1937–1941

1937 Salisbury Indians Team-Signed Baseball, Third View. The photograph at right captures the signatures of Indians business manager Melvin Murphy, John Bassler, Edgar Leip, Bill Luzansky, and Jerry Lynn. Former Parksley Spuds manager John "Poke" Whalen also signed this section of the ball.

1937 Salisbury Indians Team-Signed Baseball, Fourth View. The autographs in this image include those of star pitchers Frank Trechock and Joe Kohlman as well as those of front-office staff members.

KEN RAFFENSBERGER. In this photograph, Cambridge Cardinals players Charles Marshall (left) and Ken Raffensberger (right) discuss strategy before a 1937 game. Raffensberger won 18 games for Cambridge that year and went on to play with the Philadelphia Phillies, Cincinnati Reds, St. Louis Cardinals, and Chicago Cubs.

Special Instructions And
Advice To
MANAGERS, PLAYERS and
UMPIRES

Eastern Shore League

1937

These instructions are issued to assist in having a better understanding of the Eastern Shore League Rules and Regulations. It is our aim to help maintain baseball as the great American sport and maintain at all times the highest standard of skill and sportsmanship among its players.

Play Hard - Play To Win - Play Fair

J. THOMAS KIBLER, President
Chestertown, Maryland

EASTERN SHORE LEAGUE INSTRUCTION MANUAL. Issued by league president Tom Kibler in 1937, this manual was meant to assist players, managers, and umpires with the ESHL's rules and regulations.

1938 Centreville Colts. The Centreville, Maryland, team switched affiliations for the 1938 season from the Red Sox to the Phillies. Star players that year included Walt Cielesz, Carl Bethman, Walter Carroll, Ray Rist, Norm Wurst, Pete Dulick, Tom Ogden, and Wayne Lomas.

1938 Centreville Colts Ballpark. This action photograph from the Centreville Colts' 1938 season shows a billboard on the outfield fence for the Friel Lumber Company of Queenstown, Maryland—a company still in business today.

1938 CENTREVILLE COLTS. This more formal team photograph of the Centreville Colts has them wearing the uniforms of their parent club, the Philadelphia Phillies.

1938 DOVER ORIOLES SCORE CARD. Here is a well-preserved scorecard from the Dover team during the 1938 season. Star players such as George Le Gates, Vincent Christy, George Reisinger, Mike Kucinski, Alex Monchak, John Swank, and Fred Clemence led the Orioles that year. Players Monchak, Mel Bosser, Wally Millies, Mel Queen, and Dick West all eventually advanced to the major leagues.

BALL TWO: 1937–1941

1937 EASTON BROWNS. The Easton Browns, managed by Doc Jacobs, finished the 1937 season second to the pennant-winning Salisbury Indians. The 19-year-old Mickey Vernon sparked the team's offense, hitting for a .287 average, 10 home runs, and 64 RBI. Pitchers Frank Radler and Harry Kuntashian led the team in wins with 16 and 15 respectively. Vernon and future Chicago Cubs and Kansas City Royals manager Charlie Metro would each advance to the major leagues. The next year, Easton changed its name to the Easton Cubs.

<u>BOX SEAT</u>   BOX No. *8*

The Dover Baseball & Exhibition Co.
OF THE EASTERN SHORE LEAGUE

This ticket entitles the holder to One Box Seat Only
during the Season 1938

ORIOLE PARK - SEASON 1938
DOVER, DELAWARE

Harry O'Donnell

General Manager

1938 DOVER ORIOLES SEASON PASS. This is a rare 1938 season pass for one box seat at Oriole Park in Dover, Delaware, issued by the Dover Baseball and Exhibition Company. The Dover Orioles finished in fourth place for the 1938 season. Dick West had a great year with the bat, leading the team with a .434 average and 22 home runs. West later played six years with the Cincinnati Reds.

DUCKY DETWEILER. Future Boston Brave Robert "Ducky" Detweiler was the star of the Federalsburg Athletics in 1939. After his major-league career ended, Detweiler managed the Federalsburg club, and he has lived in Federalsburg ever since. A teammate of Detweiler's on the 1939 Federalsburg team was 18-year-old future major-league star Elmer Valo. (Courtesy of Ducky Detweiler.)

1939 CAMBRIDGE SEASON PASS. The season pass to the Cambridge Cardinals below was issued to Robert Matthews for the 1939 season. Matthews was the ESHL's treasurer.

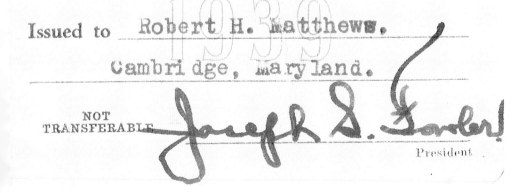

SEASON COMPLIMENTARY
Cambridge Baseball Club

1939

Issued to   Robert H. Matthews,

Cambridge, Maryland.

NOT
TRANSFERABLE   *Joseph D. Forbes*

President

1939 DUCKY DETWEILER CONTRACT. The Federalsburg Athletics paid Ducky Detweiler $75 a month during the 1939 Federalsburg season. This class-D ESHL contract was Detweiler's first of many in professional baseball. (Courtesy of Ducky Detweiler.)

No. 641

FEDERALSBURG, MD. May 20, 1939

$37.12

DAY TO THE ORDER OF Robt. Detweiler

THE SUM OF ****37 DOLS 12 CTS

DOLLARS

$8.34

TO COUNTY TRUST COMPANY OF MARYLAND

65-156 FEDERALSBURG, MD.

Donald C. Jefferson Treas.

1939 FEDERALSBURG A'S PAYCHECK. May 20, 1939, marked Ducky Detweiler's first payday in professional baseball. This original check for $37.12 from the Federalsburg Athletic Association is made out to Robert Detweiler. (Courtesy of Ducky Detweiler.)

1941 EASTERN SHORE LEAGUE OPENING DAY. The above image shows the Centreville Red Sox entering the ballpark for their game with the Cambridge Canners on opening day in 1941. Future major-league pitcher Mel Parnell was a member of the Centreville club. The photograph below shows their opponents, the Cambridge Canners, entering the ballpark on the same day. Key members of the 1941 Cambridge team included Goldy Tyler and Tom Koval.

CONSTITUTION AND
BY-LAWS

EASTERN SHORE
LEAGUE of
PROFESSIONAL
BASE BALL CLUBS

Revised As Of
APRIL 1, 1939

1939 EASTERN SHORE LEAGUE BYLAWS.
Here is a rare original copy of the Eastern
Shore League of Professional Base Ball Clubs
constitution and bylaws for the 1939 season.

1939 PLAYER RELEASE NOTICE. On
this official release notice dated July 9,
1939, Marino Joseph "Joe" Consoli was
released by the Cambridge Cardinals
and assigned to the Hamilton Redwings
of the Pennsylvania-Ontario-New York
("PONY") League. Consoli enjoyed a long
career in the minor leagues, playing until
1954 and reaching the single-A level in
the New York Yankees organization.

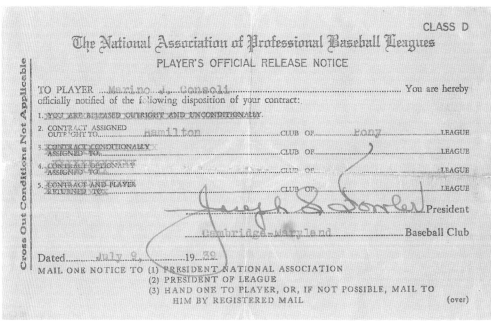

CLASS D

The National Association of Professional Baseball Leagues

PLAYER'S OFFICIAL RELEASE NOTICE

Cross Out Conditions Not Applicable

TO PLAYER ...Marino J. Consoli.. You are hereby
officially notified of the following disposition of your contract:

1. YOU ARE RELEASED OUTRIGHT AND UNCONDITIONALLY.

2. CONTRACT ASSIGNED
OUTRIGHT TO..........Hamilton.................................CLUB OF........Pony..............LEAGUE

3. CONTRACT CONDITIONALLY
ASSIGNED TO...CLUB OF..............................LEAGUE

4. CONTRACT OPTIONALLY
ASSIGNED TO...CLUB OF..............................LEAGUE

5. CONTRACT AND PLAYER
RETURNED TO..CLUB OF..............................LEAGUE

....Joseph S. Fowler..........President

........................Cambridge-Maryland...........................Baseball Club

Dated........July 9,................19..39..

MAIL ONE NOTICE TO (1) PRESIDENT NATIONAL ASSOCIATION
(2) PRESIDENT OF LEAGUE
(3) HAND ONE TO PLAYER, OR, IF NOT POSSIBLE, MAIL TO
HIM BY REGISTERED MAIL   (over)

CENTREVILLE GROUNDSKEEPER. This is a unique 1940s photograph of the Centreville Red Sox groundskeeper, nicknamed "Brownie." By all accounts, Brownie did a fine job.

1940 CAMBRIDGE CARDINALS LETTERHEAD. This is a letter for payment of a box seat at the Cambridge ballpark for the 1940 season. This box cost $10 for the entire season. Note the unique message at the top left on the letterhead that advertises "Night Baseball, Football, and Other Clean Sports."

1940 CENTREVILLE RED SOX. Here is a portrait of the 1940 second-place Centreville Red Sox. Led by future major-league pitcher Jocko Thompson (18-5), the Red Sox narrowly lost the pennant to the Dover Orioles. Other stars on the club were Troy Needham, John Jaust, Ken Butler, Albin Mocek, and Bill Thomas.

1940 CENTREVILLE LADIES. This photograph shows a women's exhibition game played at the Centreville ballpark during the 1940 season.

DOVER ORIOLES

PENNANT WINNERS EASTERN SHORE LEAGUE 1940

FRONT ROW — VOGEL - HOGAN - ZIMMERMAN - CLARK - SWOBODA - DEEGAN - PHILLIPS
BACK ROW — GALOMB - GAULIN - KARDASH - CONTINI - JAUST - TRIM - WODZICKI - DECUBELLI.

1940 DOVER ORIOLES. With a record of 72-48, the Dover Orioles won the 1940 ESHL pennant over the Centreville Red Sox. From left to right, they are (first row) Ed Vogel, Mike Hogan, Bob Zimmerman, Cap Clark, Paul Swoboda, ? Deegan, and Randall Phillips; (second row) Bill Golomb, Paul Gaulin, Mike Kardash, Bob Contini, John Jaust, Leo Trim, Ed Wodzicki, and Steve DeCubellis.

TROY NEEDHAM. Centreville Red Sox pitcher Troy Needham is seen here in 1940, when he went 12-5 with a 3.30 ERA. In 1941, Needham played for Centreville again and then pitched as Pvt. Troy Needham for the Kentucky Wildcats of the U.S. Army's 1st Armored Division in World War II. In 1946, Needham returned for one final year of professional baseball in the East Texas League.

EDDIE GAEDEL'S PREDECESSOR?
During a famous major-league game in 1951, Chicago White Sox owner Bill Veeck inserted 3-foot-7-inch Eddie Gaedel for one at-bat. This photograph was taken before a league game at Centreville in 1941, ten years before Gaedel's feat. Perhaps Veeck was in attendance and saw this fellow batting.

CENTREVILLE BASEBALL IN FLIGHT. Few images of the Eastern Shore League capture a baseball in flight, as does this one taken in the Centreville ballpark. The ball appears to have been hit pretty well.

1937 SALISBURY MANAGER JAKE FLOWERS AWARDED. Surrounded by his players, Jake Flowers is presented with his *Sporting News* 1937 Minor-League Manager of the Year award. Flowers guided the Salisbury Indians to the ESHL pennant with 59 wins after having to forfeit 21 victories earlier in the season for using an illegal player. That player, Bob Brady, went on to play for the Boston Braves in 1946 and 1947 but ended his major-league career with just one hit in six at-bats. In addition to Brady, six other members of the 1937 Salisbury Indians were called up to the major leagues, all of them with the Washington Senators.

1941

1941 CENTREVILLE RED SOX. Despite a winning record, this Centreville team ended up in fourth place. Nevertheless, several Sox enjoyed productive seasons, including pitchers Joe Ostrowski (10-4) and Gene Jones (11-4) and position players Ed Walls, John McNicholas, and Al Mathes, all of whom batted .300 or better. Ostrowski and fellow Red Sox pitcher Mel Parnell later advanced to the major leagues.

1941 MILFORD GIANTS SCHEDULE. The publishers of the *Milford Chronicle* weren't above mixing their community boostership with their marketing, as shown on the front of this Milford Giants 1941 schedule. During the second ESHL era, a number of companies supported their local teams with this sort of combination game calendar and advertisement. (Courtesy of Bob Voshell.)

ED WALLS. This fine photograph from the 1941 season shows Centreville Red Sox player Eddie Walls in his dirty uniform. Walls finished second on the team with a .321 batting average.

FRANCIS GUNNING CONTRACT. Here is an example of an Eastern Shore League uniform player's contract from the 1941 season. This particular contract paid Francis Art Gunning $100 a month to play for the Milford Giants. Gunning earned his money, batting .329 for the year. (Courtesy of the Milford Museum.)

SALISBURY MANAGER JAKE FLOWERS. Taken during the 1937 or 1938 season, this rare photograph shows Indians manager Jake Flowers casually talking to a member of an opposing team.

ED FEINBERG. This candid photograph shows Ed Feinberg playing catch before a 1937 Centreville Colts game. Hitting for a .334 average with 15 home runs and 80 RBI for the 1937 season, Feinberg went on to play for the National League's Philadelphia Phillies for parts of the 1938 and 1939 seasons. Note how full the grandstands were on this day.

1938 DOVER ORIOLES TICKET. These rain checks were issued by the Dover Baseball and Exhibition Company for a 1938 Dover Orioles game at Dover's Oriole Park.

1939 FEDERALSBURG A'S PROGRAM. Covered with local advertisements, this 1939 Federalsburg Athletics program shows how local businesses supported their ESHL teams. With future major-leaguers Ron Northey, Gene Hermanski, Joe Rullo, Jack Wallaesa, Ducky Detweiler, and Elmer Valo leading the way, the Federalsburg team won 83 games and ran away with the 1939 pennant.

Opening Day 1941. The Sudlersville Band played before Centreville's first game of the 1941 season. Lying not far from Centreville, Sudlersville is the hometown of Baseball Hall of Famer and one-time ESHL star Jimmie Foxx. Notice the billboards from local businesses lining the outfield fence.

CAMBRIDGE CANNERS. The Cambridge ball team changed its name back to the Canners for the 1940 and 1941 seasons. In this photograph, several Cambridge players lounge on a bench in what looks like a bullpen area.

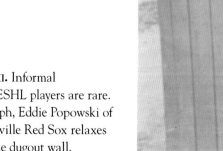

EDDIE POPOWSKI. Informal photographs of ESHL players are rare. In this photograph, Eddie Popowski of the 1941 Centreville Red Sox relaxes by leaning on the dugout wall.

FEDERALSBURG A'S SCHEDULE. This vintage schedule is from the Federalsburg Athletic Association for the Federalsburg A's during the 1937–1941 ESHL.

FEDERALSBURG ATHLETIC ASSOCIATION, INC.

SCHEDULE

of

HOME GAMES

Hall-Cross Broiler Chicks

Make More Money

▼

J. R. Eddington

Federalsburg, Md.

RIP SHILLINGFORD. Posing here in his catcher's stance is Bill "Rip" Shillingford, who played in the ESHL for Centreville and Easton during the 1937 and 1938 seasons.

JAKE FLOWERS. An award-winning manager for the Salisbury Indians in 1937, Eastern Shore native Jake Flowers also managed Salisbury in 1938 and skippered the Pocomoke City team in 1939. Flowers guided the Salisbury Indians to the ESHL pennant in both 1937 and 1938.

Uniform Agreement for the Assignment of a Player's Contract to or by a Major League Club

IMPORTANT NOTICE

Seven counterpart originals of this Agreement must be executed and mailed to the Secretary-Treasurer, Office of the Baseball Commissioner, 2901 Carew Tower, Cincinnati 2, Ohio, accompanied by a check for the consideration. If due a Minor League Club, the check shall be to the order of "The National Association of Professional Baseball Leagues"; if due a Major League Club, the check shall be to the order of that Club.

IF EXECUTED AGREEMENTS ARE NOT FILED WITH THE SECRETARY-TREASURER WITHIN 10 DAYS AFTER THE TRANSFER IS EFFECTED, HE SHALL COLLECT A PENALTY OF $50 FROM THE CLUB RESPONSIBLE, OR FROM EACH OF THE PARTIES IF BOTH CLUBS ARE RESPONSIBLE FOR THE DELAY.

This Agreement, made and entered into this ___1st___ day of ___April___ , 19_50_ .

by and between ___National League Base Ball Club of Boston___ (Party of the First Part)

and ___Milwaukee Baseball Club (American Assn)___ (Party of the Second Part)

Witnesseth: The party of the first part hereby assigns to the party of the second part the contract

of Player ___John E. Meiss nburger___

according to the Rules adopted under the Major League Agreement and the Major-Minor League Agreement and upon the following conditions (including any provisions set forth upon the back of this agreement):

On option, in consideration of the payment of one hundred dollars ($100.), with right of recall on or before October 1, 1950, on payment of the sum of five hundred dollars ($500,) by the Boston Club.

(If above space is insufficient, use back of this agreement for any additional provisions.)

In Testimony Whereof, we have subscribed hereto, through our respective Presidents or authorized agents, on the date above written:

NATIONAL LEAGUE BASE BALL CLUB OF BOSTON, Inc.   MILWAUKEE AMERICAN ASSOCIATION

_____Club   _____Club

By _____   By _____
(Party of the First Part)   (Party of the Second Part)

Corporate name of Company Club or Association of each party should be written in first paragraph and subscribed hereto.

FLOWERS-SIGNED CONTRACT.
After his stint as a manager in the ESHL, Jake Flowers served as president and general manager of the Milwaukee team in the American Association. This contract, signed by Flowers in 1950, assigns a player's contract to the Boston Braves.

Second Annual

BANQUET

of the

**Eastern Shore
Sports Writers'
Association**

held at

EASTON FIRE HOUSE

on

JIMMY FOXX

BILL NICHOLSON

TUESDAY, NOVEMBER 18, 1941

IN HONOR OF

JIMMY FOXX *and* BILL NICHOLSON

1941 EASTERN SHORE WRITERS BANQUET. In 1941, the Eastern Shore Sportswriters Association held its second annual banquet in Easton, Maryland. Jimmie Foxx was the featured ballplayer, along with Chicago Cubs slugger Bill Nicholson. Nicholson was another local boy, hailing from Chestertown, Maryland, on the Eastern Shore.

MEL PARNELL. At the time of this 1941 photograph, lefty Mel Parnell was a pitcher for the Centreville Red Sox. Parnell went on to be an outstanding pitcher for the Boston Red Sox, winning 123 games during his solid 10-year major-league career. In 1949, he led the American League with 25 wins, and he won 21 games in 1953.

1938 CENTREVILLE MANAGER JOE O'ROURKE. Centreville Colts manager Joe O'Rourke poses for this photograph in 1938. Known for his toughness, O'Rourke was once involved in a famous fight on the field with an opposing ESHL manager. As suggested by this photograph, the Colts were an affiliate of the Philadelphia Phillies.

MANAGER AND UMPIRE. In the photograph below, taken at the Centreville ballpark in the late 1930s, a team manager appears to be arguing with the umpire. This classic confrontation is a familiar scene in every baseball league, regardless of the era.

MILFORD PLAYERS. Three unidentified Milford ballplayers relax in their road uniforms around 1940.

Official Score Card

SALISBURY BASEBALL CLUB

Eastern Shore League
GORDY PARK

Season of 1937

Salisbury at Home - 1937

May 19	Cambridge	July 14, 25	Pocomoke
May 21, 29	Crisfield	July 15	Crisfield
May 25	Dover	July 23, 31	Federalsburg
May 28, 30	Federalsburg	July 24, 27	Centreville
May 31	Easton	Aug. 10, 16, 30	Crisfield
June 2, 6, 29	Centreville	Aug. 3, 21, 26	Dover
June 5, 16	Pocomoke	Aug. 6, 28	Pocomoke
June 10, 26	Dover	Aug. 13, 23	Easton
June 8, 20	Cambridge	Aug. 17, 18	Federalsburg
June 17	Crisfield	Aug. 19, 29	Centreville
June 23	Easton	Aug. 24	Cambridge
June 25	Federalsburg	Sept. 1	Pocomoke
July 1, 10, 29	Cambridge	Sept. 2	Crisfield
July 4, 7	Dover	Sept. 6	Easton
July 5, 9, 21	Easton		

Nº 5087

1937 SALISBURY INDIANS PROGRAM. This image shows an extremely rare scorecard and program from the celebrated 1937 Salisbury Indians championship season; a spectator has filled in the scorecard in this particular program. This exhibition game was played after the 1937 season at Salisbury's Gordy Park between the ESHL champions and the Philadelphia Athletics. The Salisbury nine won the exhibition 3-2.

FEDERALSBURG MASCOT SKIPPER MAGEE. The young man seen here posing for a photograph in front of two Federalsburg players was an A's mascot in 1939. Note the billboards on the Federalsburg outfield fence advertising local businesses. (Courtesy of Ducky Detweiler.)

NORM WURST. In this 1938 photograph, Centreville player Norm Wurst is seen in his Colts uniform relaxing before a ball game. It is a rare glimpse of a 1930s ESHL player in a casual pose.

POCOMOKE CITY BALLPARK. This image captures boys at play outside an ESHL ballpark during the 1930s. The Pocomoke, Maryland, stadium shown here is where the Red Sox (1937–1939) and Chicks (1940) created many memories for their fans.

1940 POCOMOKE CITY CHICKS. Future big-leaguers Carl Furillo, Gene Hermanski, and Ray Murray all played for the Pocomoke City club in 1940. The Chicks were Pocomoke's final entry in the ESHL. Managed by Poke Whalen, they finished the year with a 50-75 record, last in the eight-team league.

1938 MILFORD GIANTS TEAM-SIGNED BALL. This rare signed baseball from the Milford Giants' 1938 season includes the autograph of future major-league great Sid Gordon. Gordon led the Giants with a .352 average, slugging 25 home runs and knocking in 83 runs. Bill Lucaire, Stan Bennett, and Sid Gordon have signed the section of the ball shown at left.

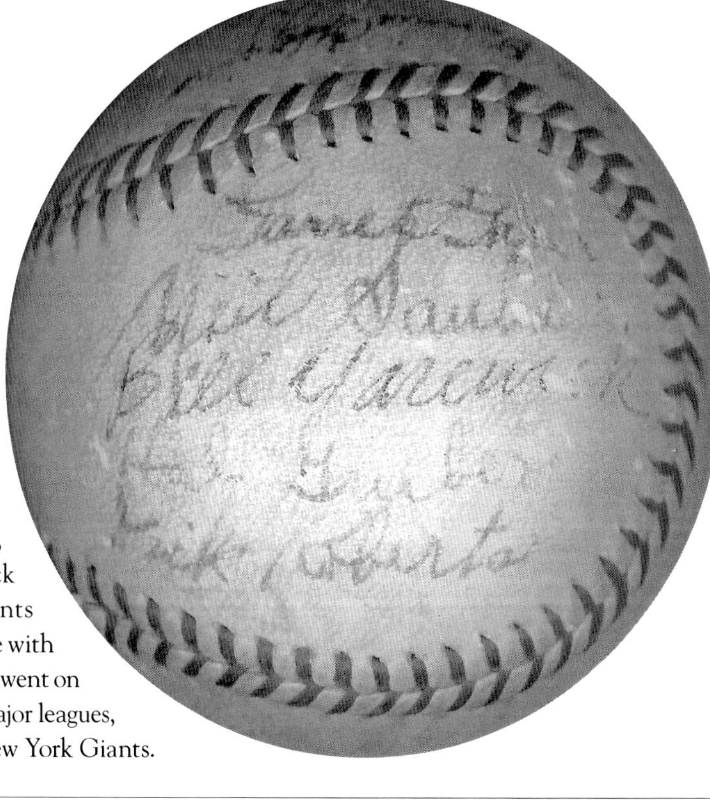

1938 MILFORD GIANTS TEAM-SIGNED BALL, SECOND VIEW. This section shows the names of Garrett Grier, Neil Saulia, Bill Yarewick, Harold Gruber, and Dick Roberts. The 1938 Giants finished third in the league with a 60-52 record. Sid Gordon went on to play 13 seasons in the major leagues, most of them with the New York Giants.

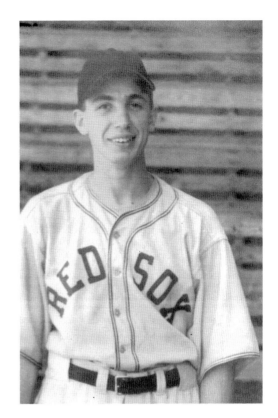

WILLIAM THOMAS. In 1940, Bill Thomas played for the Centreville Red Sox, batting .270 for the year. Thomas enlisted in the Army Air Force in 1941, earning his wings in May 1942. Having risen to second lieutenant, Thomas was killed in action in North Africa at the age of 24. In the 1940 photograph at right, Thomas is pictured in his Centreville Red Sox uniform. The photograph below shows Thomas shortly before his death. He was a baseball hero to some, an American hero to us all.

FEDERALSBURG ATHLETIC ASSOCIATION, Inc.

of the

Eastern Shore League — Class D

•

FEDERALSBURG, MARYLAND

PHONE NUMBERS:
BALL PARK 2371   BUSINESS OFFICE 3131

DR. W. K. KNOTTS
PRESIDENT

DONALD JEFFERSON
VICE PRESIDENT & TREASURER

ELBERT LIDEN
SECRETARY

DAVID SLOAN
BUSINESS MANAGER

JOSEPH O'ROURKE
MANAGER

WINTER ADDRESS
3151 ARAMINGO AVE
PHILADELPHIA, PA.

4/8/42

J. Emile Dion,
Quebec City, Canada.

Dear Sir:

I am sorry to have to advise you that we have a club — Batona N.Y. who will train here from April 15th to April 27th. We are giving them the park free of charge & room & board at the hotel is $10 per week per man for breakfast + at night a $12 for 3 meals.

If your training period does not conflict with Batona's we can offer you the same. If not I'd advise you to write Frank Luce Bus. Mgr. at Milford, Del. I'm sure they will give you the park free of any rent.

1942 FEDERALSBURG LETTER. This letter, written after the close of the 1941 season, provides a little insight as to what went on at some of the ESHL's idle ballparks after the second league ended. Dated April 1942, this letter between officers of the Federalsburg Athletic Association and a Quebec team reveals that at least a few ESHL ballparks were used for spring training by other minor-league teams from points farther north.

3

B A L L   T H R E E
1 9 4 6 – 1 9 4 9

In 1946, during the first spring after the end of World War II, Eastern Shore League baseball returned to the Delmarva Peninsula. Fred Lucas had sparked this resurrection when he asked Branch Rickey to invest money in the Cambridge ballpark. When Rickey agreed, the other ESHL teams followed Cambridge's lead, and by early 1946, the league was open for business. Towns fielding teams in the third and final ESHL were Seaford, Rehoboth Beach, Milford, and Dover, Delaware; and Easton, Cambridge, Centreville, Federalsburg, and Salisbury, Maryland.

The ESHL's last era was a memorable one. In 1946, Centreville won the pennant without a single future major-leaguer on its roster. The 1947 season was the most successful of the era, finishing with an exciting seven-game playoff series in which the Seaford Eagles defeated the pennant-winning Cambridge Dodgers to capture the league championship.

Federalsburg's Pep Rambert (.376) and Ducky Detweiler (.352) led ESHL hitters in 1947, while Bill Ripken of the Cambridge Dodgers finished with a .346 average. Cambridge pitchers Chris Van Cuyk and Carroll Beringer also enjoyed outstanding seasons, leading the league in wins with 25 and 22 victories, respectively.

Former Phillies first-baseman Gene Corbett led the Salisbury Cardinals to the pennant in 1948 after finishing last the year before. The Easton Yankees won the 1949 pennant but lost in the playoffs to the Rehoboth Beach Seahawks, who had lost their support from the Pirates after the 1948 season and were operating as an independent club.

In truth, all across the league, teams in the third ESHL suffered from diminished support from their major-league affiliates. At the end of the 1949 season, this lack of support helped finally undo the league for good. The overriding cause of the ESHL's third and final collapse, however, was its ever-lackluster ticket sales. Though Eastern Shore League baseball was exciting to watch and has never been forgotten by its faithful fans, its perennial attendance struggles made it an unprofitable proposition for club owners. When the spring of 1950 arrived, the league's turnstiles were locked and its fields abandoned. The Eastern Shore League would never return to the Delmarva Peninsula.

1946 SEAFORD EAGLES. The 1946 season was Seaford's first year as an ESHL entry. Using nearly 50 players and two different managers, the Delaware nine finished sixth in the eight-team league. Walter Youse began the year as manager and was replaced during the season by ex-big-leaguer Joe Becker. Former major-leaguer Hank Schmulback and future major-league pitcher Duke Markell were the two featured players for the young Eagles. In this photograph, Markell is fourth from the left in the third row; Becker is sixth from the left.

1946 SEAFORD EAGLES CAP. This is a rare game-worn baseball cap from the Seaford Eagles' 1946 season. Collectors today consider any piece of game-worn memorabilia from the three ESHLs a treasure.

1946 CENTREVILLE ORIOLES. The one year that Centreville entered a team in the 1946–1949 ESHL was a fruitful one: the Orioles won the pennant easily with 88 wins and 37 defeats. Former major-leaguer Jim McLeod guided the team of young players, none of whom would ever reach the major leagues.

Seaford
EAGLES
Official 1946 Schedule
of
Home Games

Eastern Shore League

1946 SEAFORD EAGLES SCHEDULE. A typical example of an ESHL team schedule, this 1946 game calendar nicely shows the Seaford logo on its front.

MILFORD RED SOX
1946

REHOBOTH BEACH PIRATES

Schedule For 1947

Eastern Shore League

1946 MILFORD RED SOX. Managed by former major-leaguer Walter Millies, the 1946 Milford Red Sox finished second to Centreville. Millies led the Sox in batting with a .353 average, and Joe Tully was the team's best pitcher, ending the season with 15 wins. Other notable players were Tom Poholsky and Grady Wilson, both of whom went on to play in the major leagues.

1947 REHOBOTH BEACH PIRATES SCHEDULE. As the front of this schedule shows, there were Pirates in Rehoboth Beach, Delaware, in 1947. During Rehoboth Beach's first year in the ESHL, the Pirates were aided by Eastern Shore native and future Pittsburgh Pirate Joe Muir. The Pirates' top starter, Muir finished the year with a 13-5 record. The Pirates finished in sixth place.

1946 CAMBRIDGE DODGERS TEAM-SIGNED BASEBALL. This rare 1946 Cambridge Dodgers–signed baseball shows, at right, the autographs of Al Leap, Hank Parker, Jean Bournot, and Merrill McDonald.

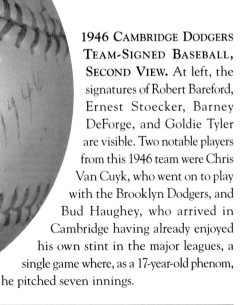

1946 CAMBRIDGE DODGERS TEAM-SIGNED BASEBALL, SECOND VIEW. At left, the signatures of Robert Bareford, Ernest Stoecker, Barney DeForge, and Goldie Tyler are visible. Two notable players from this 1946 team were Chris Van Cuyk, who went on to play with the Brooklyn Dodgers, and Bud Haughey, who arrived in Cambridge having already enjoyed his own stint in the major leagues, a single game where, as a 17-year-old phenom, he pitched seven innings.

1946 FEDERALSBURG A'S. The Athletics team above was led by 34-year-old pitcher/manager Lew Krausse, who led A's pitchers with 11 wins. Despite burning through more than 50 players by season's end, Krausse never found the right combination, and Federalsburg finished last in the league with just 37 victories.

EASTERN SHORE LEAGUE RECORD BOOK. Printed in 1947, the book at left was published by famed Eastern Shore sportswriter Ed Nichols, for many years the sports editor of the *Salisbury Times*. Full of information, statistics, photographs, and stories, this publication is a favorite among collectors.

1946 CENTREVILLE TEAM-SIGNED BASEBALL.
This mint baseball is signed by the 1946
Centreville Orioles. Signatures visible
at right are those of Al Heuser, Stan
Coulling, Mike Gast, Don Smith,
Jim Stevens, and Irv Schupp.

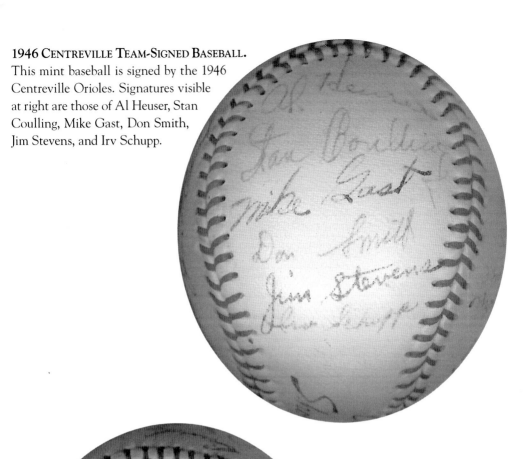

1946 CENTREVILLE TEAM-SIGNED BASEBALL, SECOND VIEW. At left, the autographs of Bill Dornbusch, George Cave, Nick Malfara, Ray Holton, and Jim McLeod can be seen. Although none of the 1946 Centreville Orioles made it to the major leagues, the team's pitching staff was very good. Dick Waldt and Stan Coulling won 17 games each, while Gast, Cave, and Smith won 16, 14, and 11 games respectively.

EASTERN SHORE LEAGUE

79

1946 SALISBURY CARDINALS. Manager Harold Contini's team featured 17-year-old future big-leaguer Steve Bilko. From left to right are (first row) August Mormino, Sylvester Rewczuk, manager Harold Contini, Jerome Cunningham, Paul Porubiski, and Charles DiCola; (second row) John Harper, Steve Bilko, Carl Wollgast, Ray Weiss, Greg Masson, and Howard Palmer; (third row) business manager C. Whamsley, Stubby Brown, Harold Sharp, Charles Miller, Bob Howe, Sid Langston, and Remy LeBlanc.

1945 STOCK CERTIFICATE. Here is a fine example of a 1945 Milford Athletic Association stock certificate. It sold for a whopping $25 per share. (Courtesy of the Milford Museum.)

DUCKY DETWEILER. After his major-league career ended, Robert "Ducky" Detweiler returned to play and manage in the ESHL for the Federalsburg A's. Detweiler played in the league from 1947 to 1949, winning the league's most valuable player award in 1947, batting .352, slugging 29 home runs, and driving in 133 runs. Detweiler played for and managed the Federalsburg nine for the 1948 season, batting .341 with 21 home runs and 95 RBI. (Courtesy of Ducky Detweiler.)

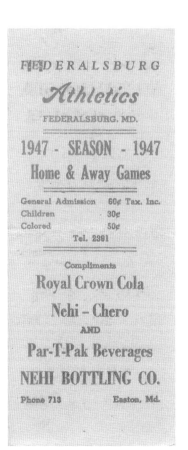

1947 FEDERALSBURG A'S SCHEDULE. In perfect condition, this schedule is from the 1947 Federalsburg A's. On the front, the schedule has the ticket prices along with an advertisement for a local business. Inside is Federalsburg's schedule for the entire season.

Salisbury Cardinals, Inc.

Official Score Card

Phone 1031-J   FIVE CENTS

WEST'S

SALISBURY'S
PRAYER
TO
FINE FOODS

WEST'S RESTAURANT
Cor. E. Main & Popular
Hill Avenue
SALISBURY, MARYLAND

1946 SALISBURY CARDINALS SCORECARD. For a mere 5¢, the Salisbury faithful used scorecards like this one to keep track of their favorite Cardinal team in 1946. This program also features vintage local advertisements.

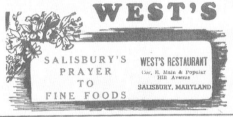

COMPLIMENTARY

SALISBURY CARDINALS

Issued to

Acct.

BUSINESS MANAGER

SALISBURY CARDINALS TICKET. Although aged quite a bit, this ticket shows that even back in the 1940s, free tickets were given out. This complimentary pass was issued by the business manager of the Salisbury Cardinals.

1946 Seaford Eagles Team-Signed Baseball. This baseball is fairly unique because, as seen at right, it features the signature of Seaford Eagles manager Walter Youse, who was replaced with Joe Becker halfway through the 1946 season. (Courtesy of Ben Peterson.)

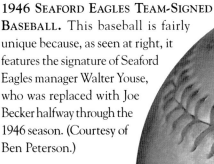

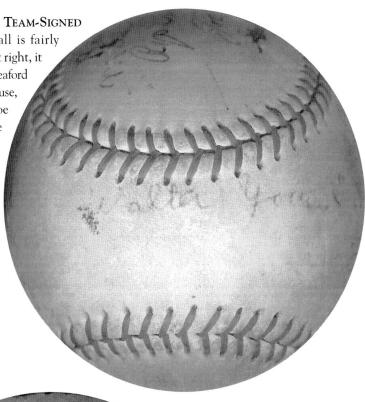

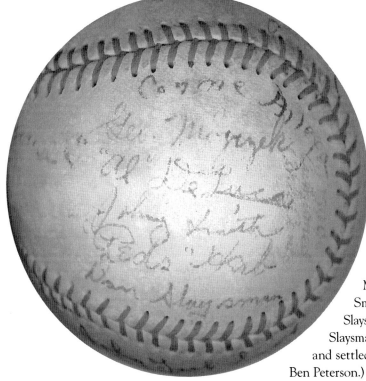

1946 Seaford Eagles Team-Signed Baseball, Second View. The photograph at left shows the signatures of Connie Allego, George Mlyczek, Al DeLuca, John Smith, Bob Herb, and Dan Slaysman. DeLuca, Mlyczek, and Slaysman all married local women and settled in Seaford. (Courtesy of Ben Peterson.)

CAMBRIDGE

BASEBALL

SCHEDULE

1947

1947 CAMBRIDGE DODGERS. This Cambridge Dodgers team won the 1947 ESHL pennant only to lose to Seaford in the playoffs in seven games. Former major-leaguer Roy Nichols batted .355 for the Dodgers and drove in 130 runs. Future major-league pitcher Chris Van Cuyk led the team with 25 wins, and fellow hurler Carroll Beringer won 22. Bill Ripken (brother of Cal Ripken Sr. and uncle to Cal Jr. and Billy) is standing second from the right in the third row.

1947 CAMBRIDGE SCHEDULE. Pictured here is a fairly nondescript schedule for the 1947 pennant-winning Cambridge Dodgers.

PIRATES SCORECARD. The 1947 Rehoboth Beach Pirates offered this animated scorecard for the entire season. This is a very nice example of a vintage scorecard, with advertisements for many local businesses.

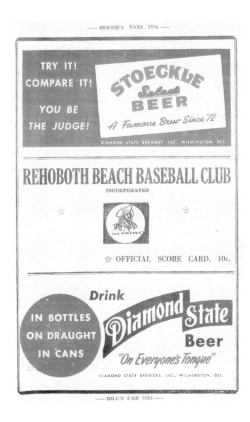

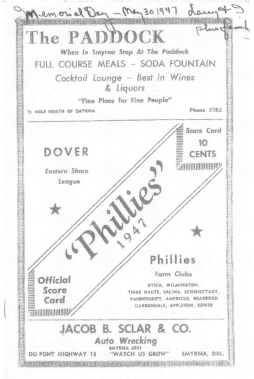

PHILLIES PROGRAM. Another fine example of a program from the ESHL, this 1947 Dover Phillies program from Memorial Day has been scored by a fan. With lots of advertisements inside, this program also lists all of the Philadelphia Phillies minor-league clubs on the cover. Guided by manager Dick Carter, the Phillies finished the year in third place with a 68-57 record.

1948 SALISBURY CARDINALS. Managed by former Philadelphia Phillies first-baseman Gene Corbett, the Salisbury Cardinals went from a last-place finish in 1947 to winning the ESHL pennant in 1948 with a 89-32 record. One of the team's strengths was its pitching rotation: future major-league hurler Herb Moford led the Cards in wins with 20; Carl Wollgast, Edward Black, and Richard Pizzo won 17, 16, and 15 games respectively. In this photograph, manager Gene Corbett stands on the right end in the third row.

1948 SALISBURY CARDINALS SCORECARD. This is the scorecard that the Salisbury Cardinals sold during their pennant-winning 1948 season. The front features a nice example of the Cardinals logo. Notice that the price of the team's scorecard (10¢) has doubled since 1946.

1947 SEAFORD EAGLES. Displayed here are two team portraits taken of the Eagles over the course of the 1947 season. This team, which would win the league championship by beating Cambridge in seven games, featured future major-leaguers Nick Testa (Giants), John Andre (Cubs), and Duke Markell (Browns), all of whom contributed to the Eagles' victory. Testa in particular was a fan favorite. Above, Markell stands in the back, third from the left. Andre is also in back, fourth from the right. Testa kneels front and center, wearing his catcher's mitt.

FEDERALSBURG ATHLETICS. Above is a very nice team photograph of the 1948 Federalsburg A's. At the helm of the A's that year was Ducky Detweiler, who led the team with a .341 average while walloping 21 home runs and driving in 95 RBI. Future major-leaguer Spider Wilhelm was also a member of this team. Note the Milford-area billboards in the background, which confirm that this photograph was taken at the Milford Red Sox's ballpark in Milford, Delaware. (Courtesy of Ducky Detweiler.)

1948 FEDERALSBURG SCORECARD. Advertisements galore are on the cover and inside of this 1948 Federalsburg A's scorecard, where several local businesses sponsored the scorecard and donated prizes for a drawing held between innings.

1948 REHOBOTH BEACH PIRATES SCORECARD. The Rehoboth Beach Baseball Club produced this scorecard for the Pirates' 1948 season.

1948 Salisbury Cardinals. This photograph shows the Cardinals receiving their awards for winning the 1948 ESHL pennant. Manager Gene Corbett stands on the far left.

LEON F. TRIVITS, *President*
Business Phone 3244
Residence Phone 3-6012

GALEN L. MILLER, *Business Manager*
Park Phone 3238
Residence Phone 2173

SEAFORD   EAGLES

Seaford Baseball Club, Inc.

EASTERN SHORE LEAGUE
SEAFORD, DELAWARE

Seaford Eagles Letterhead. The Seaford team was called the Eagles from 1946 to 1949 and used an eagle as its logo. This colorful letterhead was very stylish for the time.

Eastern Shore League NEWS

CLASS D BASE BALL AT IT'S BEST

CAMBRIDGE
FEDERALSBURG
SEAFORD

REHOBOTH
EASTON
SALISBURY

VOL. 1 — NO. 1   AUGUST, 1949   EASTERN SHORE

Shore League Race Is Tightest Ever

SIX - TEAM LOOP IS GOING GOOD, 'ORPHANS' HOT

Eastern Shore League fans were treated to something different this season during the first two months of the 120-game schedule. Usually accustomed to watching a runaway race, the 1949 season presented one of the hottest fights in the history of the ancient Class D circuit.

All six clubs went neck and neck during the first month of play with only five games separating the cellar team from the top of the loop.

Fred Lucas

Rehoboth, Salisbury, and finally Easton all took turns occupying first place in this knock-down-drag-out battle.

Those surprising Rehoboth Sea Hawks clung to first place just one month, taking over the top perch May 10th before being removed June 15th by the Salisbury Red Birds.

Manager Jack Farmer's high spirited Easton Yankees, loaded with fence-busting sluggers, moved out in front, June 21, and maintained a commanding grip as late as June 12th by seven and half lengths. The Little Yankees broke the backs of the Salisbury flock with successive wins, June 30 and 31, by identical scores of 9 to 4.

The healthiest sign in the league is the operation of the league's two independent clubs — the sharp-clawed Rehoboth Sea Hawks, and the on-rushing Federalsburg Feds. These two towns have thrown sharp challenges in the direction of major league clubs that have strong affiliations in the Sho' circuit.

1937-48 COMPOSITE EASTERN SHORE LEAGUE STANDINGS

Club	Years	Wins	Losses	Pct.	Playoff Pennants	Playoff Wins
Cambridge	8	504	425	.542	1	1
Salisbury	8	494	436	.531	3	3
Seaford	3	188	187	.501	0	1
Easton	8	445	483	.469	0	1
Federalsburg	8	431	505	.460	1	0
Rehoboth	2	109	140	.434	0	0

'NOBODY'S MOVING US OUT OF LEAD', SAYS EASTON PILOT JACK FARMER

The Easton Yanks were resting on a juicy six game first place lead, August 1st, "and they can't budge us now," beamed Manager Jack Farmer, "we're a cinch to win the pennant."

Jack Farmer

The little Yankee skipper, a slow, drawling, congenial chap from London, Ky., meant just that although he usually doesn't make such confident chatter unless he has a basis for such optimism.

Easton is judged to have the better balanced team of the loop — hitting, fielding and pitching. There isn't a weak spot anywhere, according to loyal Talbot County rooters.

Furthermore, Manager Farmer is driving his lads with that old "go get 'em" spirit. The Little Yankees are an interesting club to watch.

Some of the better pitching prospects of the New York Yankee farm system are on the roster. They include Lou Job, Wally Burnette, Andy DeAngelo, Pat Foley, Bob Hustis, and lefthanders Buddy Gebhart and Bobby Allison. Everyone is capable of stepping to the firing line for a nine inning performance.

Easton has probably the best catcher of the loop in Larry (Andy) Anderson, a .359 hitter, who blends a strong throwing whip with plenty of hustle.

Loyal fans claim there isn't a rival shortstop to carry the glove of George Priggee, a big husky kid, who moves about the short patch sector with a good pair of hands and a strong arm. Another valuable addition was third sacker Buddy Carter of Jacksonville, Fla., who brought along a booming bat from the Beaumont Texas (AA) League club. Ernie Wingard, a timely left handed hitter, plugged up a gap at second base. Dick Yata is going great guns at the getaway sack.

The heavy hitting of the Little Yankees has been delivered by the outfielders Jim Engleman, Forrest Samson, and Gordon Bragg. All are rapping the potato at a steady tempo well over the .314 circle.

Now you can see why Manager Farmer says he's enjoying plenty of restful sleep, despite the hot weather. "It's probably the best Class D club I've ever managed," he volunteered. Jack has piloted some mighty competent "D" teams, too. His tour includes Fostoria Ohio State League; Stroudsburg, Pa., North Atlantic; and Albuquerque, N. Mex., West Texas—New Mexico League.

1949 EASTERN SHORE LEAGUE NEWSLETTER. This is a very rare original copy of the *Eastern Shore League News*. The four-page foldout brims with feature articles, photographs, and statistics. Unfortunately, the August 1949 Volume One, Issue One edition would be the newsletter's only issue. The ESHL shut down for its third and final time soon after this newsletter appeared.

CLASS D

UNIFORM PLAYER'S CONTRACT
APPROVED BY THE

NATIONAL ASSOCIATION
OF
PROFESSIONAL BASEBALL LEAGUES

IMPORTANT NOTICES

The attention of both Club and Player is specifically directed to the following excerpt from Rule 3 (a), of the Major-Minor League Rules:
"No Club shall make a contract different from the uniform contract and no club shall make a contract containing a non-reserve clause, except permission be first secured from the . . . President of the National Association. The making of any agreement between a Club and Player not embodied in the contract shall subject both parties to discipline."
A copy of this contract when executed must be delivered to player either in person or by registered mail, return receipt requested.

SALARY CERTIFICATE

This Contract will not be approved by the President of the National Association unless the Salary Certificate set forth below is executed by both the Club Official concerned and the Player.

Ben Myer

Name of Club Official

Title

of the _____ club, and *Russell Hansen*

Name of Club

Name of Player

the player, each does hereby certify that all of the compensation player *Russell Hansen* is receiving, or has been promised in the form of salary, transportation (except transportation expense for one person from the player's home or point of departure to the city in which he is directed to report), allowance or bonus of whatsoever nature from any club, person, agent, organization or corporation during the life of this Agreement or thereafter or has been paid prior to the execution of said contract, if incident to the signing thereof, by any club, person, agent, organization or corporation is set forth in the contract to which this certificate is attached.

We, and each of us execute this certificate with full knowledge that if its contents be found false, the club and the undersigned player may each be fined an amount not in excess of Five Hundred Dollars ($500.00) and the president and/or the undersigned official may be suspended from participation in National Association affairs and/or the undersigned player suspended, for a period of not to exceed two (2) years from the date the decision is rendered finding said certificate to be false, all as the President of the National Association may determine.

Russell Hansen

PLAYER

W. K. Knott

AUTHORIZED OFFICIAL OF CLUB

1946 FEDERALSBURG A'S CONTRACT. This is an original ESHL uniform player's contract between the Federalsburg Athletics and Russell Hansen, signed by both the player and an A's officer.

OFFICIAL
BASE BALL SCHEDULE
SEAFORD EAGLES

HOME AND VISITING
GAMES

CITIES
SERVICE

Season of 1947
EASTERN SHORE LEAGUE

1947 SEAFORD EAGLES SCHEDULE. This trifold 1947 Seaford Eagles schedule features a superb logo on the front as well as the league name and an advertisement for a local business. The Eagles were a New York Giants affiliate in 1947 and brought home the ESHL championship, defeating the pennant-winning Cambridge team in a seven-game playoff.

1946 Salisbury Cardinals Team-Signed Baseball. Here is a rare signed baseball from the 1946 Salisbury Cardinals, with future major-leaguer Steve Bilko's autograph on it. Bilko was a 17-year-old when he played 122 games for Salisbury. The image at right shows the signatures of Steve Bilko, Edward Brown, and manager Harold Contini.

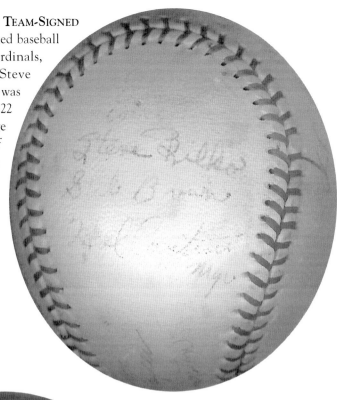

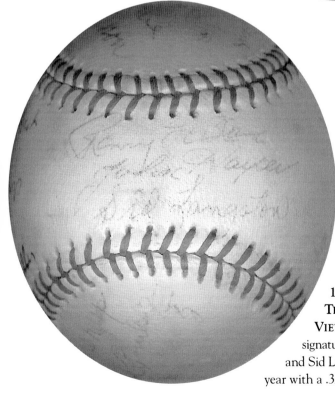

1946 Salisbury Cardinals Team-Signed Baseball, Second View. The image at left shows the signatures of Remy LeBlanc, John Harper, and Sid Langston, who led the ESHL that year with a .353 batting average.

June 14, 1949

George M. Trautman,
Columbus, Ohio.

Dear Sir:

You will find enclosed the signed contract, with its trans-
mittal, of Herman S. Smith Jr.. Please sent me the Classification of
this player.

Also enclosed is the Disability Notice of Kenneth Donnelly.

I have never received the Assignment Papers on Russell
Hansen. This Player was assigned to us outright (no sale price)
by the Wilmington, N.C. Club, subject to the option of the Waterbury
Club. I have notified both clubs(about a week ago) that I had never
received the assignment papers on this player. However, to date nothing
has been done about it. The Players' copy of his Disposition is dated
May 30, 1949. He arrived here on May 31, 1949 and was placed under our
contract on this latter date.

Very truly yours,

W.K.Knotts, Bus.Mgr.

cc Pres. Lucas.

1948 CAMBRIDGE DODGERS.
Former major-leaguer Stew Hofferth managed the Dodgers before Robert Vickery replaced him. The team finished in fourth place with a record of 65-61. Future major-leaguers on the squad were Don Nicholas (White Sox) and Gale Wade (Cubs). (Courtesy of Clifford Collison.)

1949 FEDS LETTER. At left is a note from Federalsburg's business manager to the office of Minor League Baseball. The Federalsburg team took the name "Feds" for the ESHL's last year. They finished in second place to the Easton Yankees. (Note the name of the Feds' assistant business manager: Robert "Ducky" Detweiler. The star of Federalsburg's 1939 team had rejoined the club in 1947 after stints with the Boston Braves and the U.S. Army.)

Office Of
BALDASKB.XGUDVER
President
Seaford, Del.

FRED LUCAS, President
Cambridge, Maryland

February 28, 1949

Mr. G. M. Trautman, President
National Association
696 East Broad Street
Columbus, Ohio

Dear Mr. Trautman:-

These Eastern Shore League players we are transferring to
the Federalsburg Club are off the Dover Club, which disbanded
and according to Article 29-section 30.13 under the rules
and regulations of the National Association these players
revert to the League.

The Federalsburg Club is operating independently and had quite
a time getting reorganized and this is one of the reasons for
the lateness in that Club selecting these players, but the
directors of our league felt they would like to help as much
as they could in the way of players' help and also to make
them as financially sound as possible and therefore voted to
waive the consideration fee of course, providing this meets
with your approval of which I spoke to you in New York at the
Zone 1 President's Meeting, February 6. The Federalsburg
Club is forwarding you the National Association fee and we hope
this will be satisfactory to you. Also, I am enclosing copies
of letters to the boys. Do the other players on the Dover
Reserve list have to be notified or are they automatically
free agents as of March 1st?

Very truly yours,

Fred Lucas

FRED LUCAS, President
Eastern Shore League

FL:h

MEMBER OF THE NATIONAL ASSOCIATION OF PROFESSIONAL BASEBALL LEAGUES

1949 EASTERN SHORE LEAGUE LETTER. This is a rare and very candid letter to the president of
Minor League Baseball from ESHL president Fred Lucas. The date is February 1949, and Lucas
discusses the transfer of players from the failed Dover club to Federalsburg. After Dover folded,
the Phillies moved their affiliation to the Seaford Eagles for the league's final season in 1949.

OFFICIAL EASTERN SHORE LEAGUE SCHEDULE FOR 1947

	At Cambridge	At Rehoboth	At Dover	At Easton	At Federalsburg	At Milford	At Salisbury	S
ambridge	I. G. BURTON & CO., Inc. MILFORD	May 9-22 June 4-22 July 8-15 Aug. 3-15 Sept. 5	May 20 June 1-16-29 July 11-27 Aug. 9-24 Sept. 3	May 18-30 June 6-20 July 13-24-31 Aug. 10-31	May 11-26 June 8-18 July 4-20-29 Aug. 17 Sept. 1	May 17-29 June 15-30 July 10-17 Aug. 7-22 Sept. 7	May 13 June 3-13-24 July 3-21 Aug. 13-19-26	May June July Aug.
ehoboth	May 8-23 June 5-23 July 7-16 Aug. 2-14 Sept. 4	CARS & TRUCKS	May 13 June 2-12-25 July 13-21 Aug. 11-19 Sept. 1	May 10-29 June 8-18 July 2-19-29 Aug. 17-26	May 14-25 June 10-27 July 5-25 Aug. 4-21-29	May 19-30 June 7-20 July 4-23-31 Aug. 12-31	May 21-31 June 16-28 July 12-28 Aug. 9-25 Sept. 2	May June July Aug. Sept.
over	May 21-31 June 17-28 July 12-28 Aug. 8-25 Sept. 2	May 12 June 3-13-24 July 14-22 Aug. 10-18 Sept. *1	SCHOOL BUSSES	May 17-26 June 14-30 July 9-18 Aug. 6-22 Sept. 7	May 19-28 June 7-20 July 7-23-31 Aug. 15-31	May 8-23 June 5-22 July 2-16 Aug. 2-14-20	May 15-24 June 11-26 July 5-25 Aug. 4-20-29	May June July Aug. Sept.
aston	May 19-*30 June 7-21 July 14-23 Aug. 1-11-30	May 11-28 June 9-19 July 3-20-30 Aug. 16-27	May 16-27 June 15 July 1-10-17 Aug. 7-23 Sept. 6	GENUINE PARTS	May 21 June 1-16-25 July 12-21 Aug. 8-25 Sept. 5	May 14-25 June 10-27 July 5-25 Aug. 4-21-29	May 8-23 June 5-23 July *4-16 Aug. 2-14 Sept. *1	May June July Aug. Sept.
ederalsburg	May 10-27 June 9-19 July *4-19-30 Aug 16 Sept. *1	May 15-24 June 11-26 July 6-26 Aug. 5-20-28	May 18-29 June 6-21 July 8-24 Aug. 1-12-30	May 20-31 June 17-24 July 11-22 Aug. 9-24 Sept. 4	BEAR WHEEL & FRAME ALIGNMENT	May 13 June 2-12-28 July 13-28 Aug. 10-19 Sept. 2	May 17-*30 June 14-30 July 10-17 Aug. 7-22 Sept. 6	May June July Aug.
ilford	May 16-28 June 14 July 1-9-18 Aug 6-23 Sept. 6	May 18-*30 June 6-24 July *4-24 Aug. 1-13-30	May 9-22 June 4-23 July 3-15 Aug. 3-15-27	May 15-24 June 11-26 July 6-26 Aug. 5-20-21	May 12 June 3-13-29 July 14-27 Aug. 11-18 Sept. 3	CERTIFIED MECHANICS	May 10-26 June 9-19 July 8-19-30 Aug. 16 Sept. 5	May June July Aug. Sept.
lisbury	May 12 June 2-12-25 July 2-22 Aug. 12-18-27	May 20 June 1-17-29 July 11-27 Aug. 8-24 Sept. 3	May 14-25 June 10-27 July 6-26 Aug. 5-21-28	May 9-22 June 4-22 July 4-15 Aug. 3-15 Sept. 1	May 16-30 June 15 July 1-9-18 Aug. 6-23 Sept. 7	May 11-27 June 8-18 July 7-20-29 Aug. 17 Sept. 4	SERVICE THAT REALLY SERVES	May June July Aug.
aford	May 14-24 June 10-27 July 5-25 Aug. 4-21-29	May 16-26 June 14 July 1-9-18 Aug. 6-23 Sept. 7	May 11-30 June 9-18 July 4-19-29 Aug. 17 Sept. 5	May 12 June 3-13-28 July 7-27 Aug. 13-18 Sept. 3	May 9-23 June 5-22 July 2-16 Aug. 2-15-27	May 21 June 1-16-25 July 12-21 Aug. 8-25 Sept. 1	May 19-28 June 7-20 July 14-23-31 Aug. 11-30	57
	(*) Holiday	Night Games						

1947 EASTERN SHORE LEAGUE SCHEDULE. This compact chart held the complete 1947 schedule for the entire eight-team league. Ironically, while the ESHL is long gone, the Milford Chevrolet dealership that sponsored this 1947 league schedule was still in business in 2010.

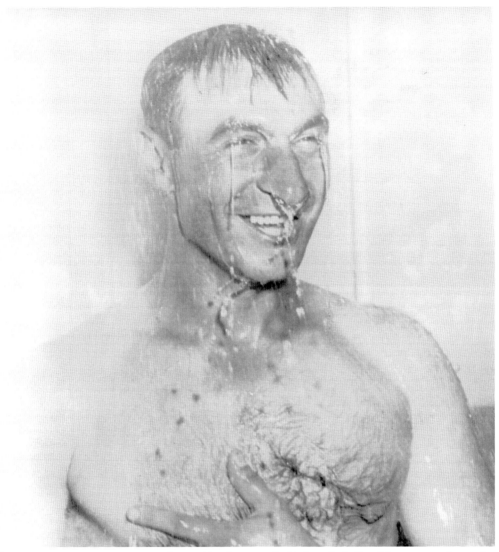

PITCHER DUKE MARKELL. In this 1950s photograph, Duke Markell celebrates a no-hitter he threw for Rochester in the International League. Markell starred in the ESHL for Seaford in 1946, 1947, and 1949.

CAMBRIDGE DODGER PENCIL. This very rare pencil from 1947 has the Cambridge Dodgers' schedule printed on it. The pencil also finds room to advertise a local business.

CAMBRIDGE DODGERS TICKETS. Eastern Shore League tickets are hard to find, but this immaculate string of Cambridge Dodgers tickets from the late 1940s is in perfect condition. Paying just 65¢ to watch a professional baseball game was certainly a bargain, even 60 years ago.

Compliments

CAMBRIDGE

DODGERS

CAMBRIDGE DODGERS MIRROR. This is perhaps the rarest of all ESHL memorabilia in existence: a small pocket mirror featuring the compliments of the Cambridge Dodgers on the reverse side.

EASTERN SHORE LEAGUE RECORD BOOK. Sportswriter Ed Nichols published two record books in the 1940s, the first in 1947 and this version in 1948. Full of statistics, stories, and photographs, this is a collectable much desired by minor-league aficionados.

EASTON YANKEES BASEBALL TOKEN. This is a 1940s token from the Easton Baseball Club of Talbot County. The Easton Yankees may have used these tokens for season passes.

Sherwood Marvel, Jess Moneymaker, Stuart Sargent and Wink Booth, Seaford baseball fans, discuss probable outcome of evening's game.

SEAFORD EAGLES BASEBALL FANS. This image is a very nice photograph of, from left to right, Seaford Eagles supporters Sherwood Marvel, Jess Moneymaker, Stuart Sargent, and Wink Booth standing in front of the post office in Seaford, Delaware. These men are possibly discussing the baseball game between the Cambridge Dodgers and the Eagles scheduled for later that night. Note the late starting time for the game.

SALISBURY MANAGER GENE CORBETT. Gene Corbett managed and played in the ESHL at Salisbury. This photograph is from the late 1930s, when Corbett was a member of the Philadelphia Phillies major-league team.

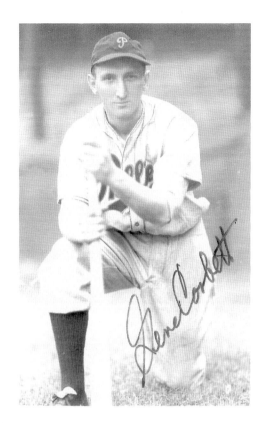

IMPORTANT NOTICE

The attention of both Club and Player is specifically directed to the following excerpt from Major League Rule 3(a):

"No Club shall make a contract different from the uniform contract or a contract containing a non-reserve clause, except with the written approval of the Advisory Council. All contracts shall be in duplicate and the Player shall retain a counterpart original. The making of any agreement between a Club and Player not embodied in the contract shall subject both parties to discipline by the Commissioner; and no such agreement, whether written or verbal, shall be recognized or enforced by the Commissioner."

National League of Professional Baseball Clubs
UNIFORM PLAYER'S CONTRACT

Parties   The PHILADELPHIA NATIONAL LEAGUE CLUB
             herein called the Club, and GENE CORBETT
             of ST. PAUL, MINNESOTA   herein called the Player.

Recital   The Club is a member of the National League of Professional Baseball Clubs. As such, and jointly with the other members of the League, it is a party to the National League Constitution and to agreements in high standards of personal conduct, of fair play and good sportsmanship.

Agreement   In view of the facts above recited the parties agree as follows:

Employment   1. The Club hereby employs the Player to render skilled service as a baseball player in connection with all games of the Club during the year 193 6 including the Club's training season, the Club's exhibition games, the Club's playing season, and the World Series (or any other official series in which the Club may participate and in any receipts of which the player may be entitled to share); and the player covenants that he will perform with diligence and fidelity the service stated and such duties as may be required of him in such employment.

Salary   2. For the service aforesaid the Club will pay the Player an aggregate salary of $ 150.00 PER MONTH ONE HUNDRED AND FIFTY DOLLARS, as follows:

             In semi-monthly installments after the commencement of the playing season covered by this contract, unless the Player is "abroad" with the Club for the purpose of playing games, in which event the amount then due shall be paid on the first week-day after the return "home" of the Club, the terms "home" and "abroad" meaning, respectively, at and away from the city in which the Club has its baseball field.

             If a monthly salary is stipulated above, it shall begin with the commencement of the Club's playing season (or such subsequent date as the Player's services may commence) and end with the termination of the Club's scheduled playing season, and shall be payable in semi-monthly installments as above provided.

             If the Player is in the service of the Club for part of the playing season only, he shall receive such proportion of the salary above mentioned, as the number of days of his actual employment in the Club's playing season bears to the number of days in said season.

Loyalty   3. (a) The Player will faithfully serve the Club or any other Club to which, in conformity with the agreements above recited, this contract may be assigned, and pledges himself to the American public to conform to high standards of personal conduct, of fair play and good sportsmanship.

             (b) The Player represents that he does not, directly or indirectly, own stock or have any financial interest in the ownership or earnings of any Major League club, except as hereinafter expressly set forth, and covenants that he will not hereafter, while connected with any Major League club, acquire or hold any such stock or interest except in accordance with Major League Rule 20 (e).

Service   4. (a) The Player agrees that, while under contract or reservation, he will not play baseball (except post-season games as hereinafter stated) otherwise than for the Club or a Club assignee hereof; that he will not engage in professional boxing or wrestling; and that, except with the written consent of the Club or its assignee, he will not engage in any game or exhibition of football, basketball, hockey or other athletic sport.

Post-season (b) The Player agrees that, while under contract or reservation, he will not play in any post-season
Games   baseball games except in conformity with the Major League Rules; and that he will not play in any such baseball game more than ten days after the close of the Major League championship season any year covered by this contract, until the following training season, or in which more than two other players of the Club participate, or with or against any ineligible player or team.

Assignment   5. (a) In case of assignment of this contract to another Club, the Player shall promptly report to the assignee club within 72 hours from the date he receives written notice from the Club of such assignment, if not more than 1600 miles by most-direct available railroad route, plus an additional 24 hours for each additional 800 miles; accrued salary shall be payable when he so reports; and such successive assignee shall become liable to the Player for his salary during his term of service with such assignee, and the Club shall not

GENE CORBETT'S CONTRACT. In 1936, Gene Corbett signed this original contract to play for the National League's Philadelphia Phillies. Corbett was paid $150 a month to be a big-league ballplayer that year.

GEORGE MCPHAIL. Seen running off the field here is George Mcphail of the Seaford Eagles. Mcphail won 26 games pitching for Seaford in 1948 and 1949.

SEAFORD EAGLES BALLPARK. The rare action photograph below was taken during a Seaford Eagles game. The umpire has this play covered.

GORDY PARK. The Salisbury Cardinals played their games in this ballpark. This is a nice view from inside Gordy Park looking at the outfield fence, which sports advertisements from local businesses.

1949 PLAYER DISPOSITION FORM. Signed by league president Fred Lucas, this player disposition form for Leonard Baker out-rights his contract to the Federalsburg team in the ESHL. Baker pitched for Dover in 1946 and 1947. After signing with Federalsburg in 1949, Baker won 14 games for the Feds.

SEAFORD TRYOUTS. This photograph shows how many baseball hopefuls would try out for an ESHL team. This tryout was held at the Seaford Eagles' ballpark. Notice the advertisement for the Peninsula Oil Company on the fence at the far right; this Seaford-based company was still in business in 2010.

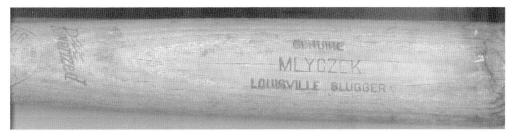

GEORGE MLYCZEK. George Mlyczek was a Seaford Eagle in 1946, hitting .303 in his only year in the ESHL. Mlyczek played minor-league baseball for three years and retired with a career batting average of .306. Mlyczek then settled down in Seaford and lived there for the rest of his life. This is an image of a game-used George Mlyczek baseball bat.

1948 MILFORD RED SOX TICKET. This is a ticket stub for the Milford Red Sox from the 1948 season. In perfect condition, this ticket is a very nice collectable from the Milford Baseball Club.

CATCHER NICK TESTA. Nick Testa was a 19-year-old catcher for the Seaford Eagles in 1947 and played minor-league baseball for 16 seasons. Testa was called up to the San Francisco Giants in their first year on the west coast in 1958, playing in one major-league game. The photograph at left captures Testa when he was playing for the Seaford Eagles in 1947. The photograph below shows him in his 1958 San Francisco Giants uniform.

TESTA IN JAPAN. Former Seaford Eagles catcher Nick Testa traveled to Japan to play professional baseball in 1962. In this photograph, Testa poses with a Japanese friend. (Courtesy of Ann Adams.)

1947 EASTON YANKEES TEAM PHOTOGRAPH. Manager Joe Antolick was a member of the 1944 Philadelphia Phillies before guiding the Easton Yankees to a seventh-place finish in the 1947 ESHL. Easton Yankees with .300 averages that year were Don Maxa, John Drew, Frank Kempf, and Antolick. Fred Prior led the pitching staff with 10 wins. (Courtesy of William Hill.)

REHOBOTH BEACH TICKET. The Rehoboth Beach Baseball Club operated in the ESHL from 1947 to 1949. The Rehoboth nine were called the Pirates in 1947 and 1948, then changed the name to the Rehoboth Beach Sea Hawks for the 1949 season. This is a rare ticket from the Rehoboth Beach club during that period.

1948 SEAFORD MANAGER SOCKS SEIBOLD. Former major-leaguer Harry "Socks" Seibold is shown at right in 1948, when he was the manager of the Seaford Eagles. After his major-league career with the Philadelphia A's and the Boston Braves was over, Seibold managed the Seaford Eagles to a sixth-place finish.

1947 SEASON PASS. Signed by league president Tom Kibler, the season pass below was issued to M. Nelson Wright. It was good for all ESHL baseball games during the 1947 season. (Courtesy of Bob Voshell.)

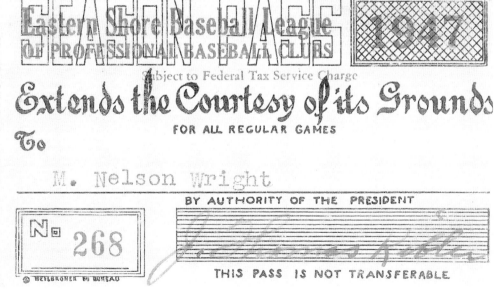

SEASON PASS
Eastern Shore Baseball League
OF PROFESSIONAL BASEBALL CLUBS
1947
Subject to Federal Tax Service Charge

Extends the Courtesy of its Grounds

FOR ALL REGULAR GAMES

To

M. Nelson Wright

BY AUTHORITY OF THE PRESIDENT

No 268

THIS PASS IS NOT TRANSFERABLE

CLASS D

OFFICIAL NOTICE OF DISPOSITION OF PLAYER'S CONTRACT AND SERVICES

National Association of Professional Baseball Leagues

MAIL ONE NOTICE AT ONCE TO: (1) President National Association.
(2) President of your League.
(3) Hand one to player. (If not possible, mail copy to player by registered mail.)
(4) Retain one copy for your files.

February 28, 1949
(Date)

TO PLAYER _____Robert Ryder_____ , You are hereby officially notified of the following disposition of your contract:

Your contract has this date been assigned outright to the Federalsburg Club of the Eastern Shore League.

Eastern Shore League   Club   Eastern Shore   League

By _Fred Lucas_   President.   (Title)

(CLUB WILL SELECT APPROPRIATE STATEMENT FROM LIST BELOW AND TYPE OR PRINT ENTIRE STATEMENT ABOVE)

DO NOT WRITE IN THIS BOX

(a) You are released outright and unconditionally.
(b) Your contract has this date been assigned outright to the _____(Club Name)_____ Club of the _____(League Name)_____ League.
(c) Your contract has this date been conditionally assigned to the _____(Club Name)_____ Club of the _____(League Name)_____ League.
(d) Your contract has this date been optionally assigned to the _____(Club Name)_____ Club of the _____(League Name)_____ League.
(e) Your contract has this date been returned to the _____(Club Name)_____ Club of the _____(League Name)_____ League.
(f) Your contract has this date been assigned outright to the _____(Club Name)_____ Club of the _____(League Name)_____ League. Subject to the option of _____(Club Name)_____ Club of the _____(League Name)_____ League.
(g) The right to recall your contract has this date been cancelled by the _____(Club Name)_____ Club of the _____(League Name)_____ League.
(h) Your contract has this date been recalled by the _____(Club Name)_____ Club of the _____(League Name)_____ League.

RECEIPT

(Date)

RECEIPT OF COPY OF THIS OFFICIAL NOTICE IS ACKNOWLEDGED

(Player)

Place X in box if player is sent copy by REGISTERED mail. ☐ PLAYER SENT COPY OF THIS OFFICIAL NOTICE BY REGISTERED MAIL.

ROBERT RYDER. This disposition form was issued by league president Fred Lucas in 1949. Robert Ryder was out-righted to the Federalsburg Feds of the ESHL. Ryder played for Dover in 1948 and in 1949 performed for both Seaford and Federalsburg.

"BIG JOHN." At 6-foot-4, John Andre pitched well in the ESHL. He won a combined 36 games for Seaford in 1947 and 1948, then transferred to Rehoboth Beach in 1949 and won another 17 games for the Sea Hawks. Andre had a cup of coffee with the Chicago Cubs in 1955. He is pictured here at the tail end of his 11-year minor-league career, playing in 1956 for the Los Angeles Angels of the AAA Pacific Coast League. That year, Andre's Angels teammate and former ESHL Salisbury Cardinals star Steve Bilko won the PCL's Triple Crown, leading the league with a .360 average, 55 home runs, and 164 RBIs.

1946 SEAFORD EAGLES JERSEY. This game-worn, pinstriped jersey was used for the Eagles' home games only. The team's away jerseys were grey with "Seaford" written across the front.

NICK TESTA MINOR-LEAGUE BAT. Vintage game-used minor league baseball bats are highly prized by collectors, and this one is no exception. Its former owner, Nick Testa, played for the Seaford Eagles in 1947 and went on to play a single inning for the major-league San Francisco Giants during their inaugural season in 1958. He later served as a strength-and-conditioning instructor for the New York Yankees.

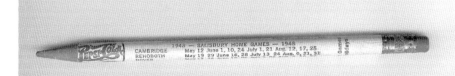

1948 Salisbury Cardinals Pencil. Advertising pencils were plentiful in the late 1940s, and this pencil with the 1948 Salisbury Cardinals' entire schedule on it was probably one of many produced. Today, however, pencils from the ESHL are quite rare.

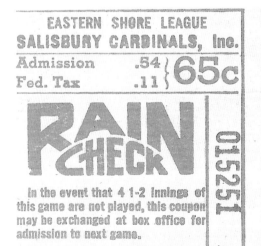

1948 Salisbury Cardinals Ticket. In very good condition, this Salisbury Cardinals ticket from the pennant-winning 1948 season has the team name printed on it as well as the league name.

SEAFORD EAGLES COLLAGE. This unusual collage from the 1947 Seaford Eagles' championship season features three future major-leaguers in John Andre (Cubs), Duke Markell (Browns), and Nick Testa (Giants).

SEAFORD EAGLES BALLPARK. Below is a rare image from the outfield looking in at the Seaford Eagles ballpark. Apparently, a pretty good crowd was on hand for this late-1940s contest.

UMPIRE JIM HONOCHICK. Jim Honochick umpired in the ESHL for the 1946 season and went on to work in the major leagues from 1949 to 1972. After retiring, Honochick was seen in the famous Miller Lite commercials on television. In this photograph, he appears to be calling Philadelphia A's speedster Spook Jacobs safe at home.

CHRIS VAN CUYK. Below, in a wire photograph taken during spring training with the Brooklyn Dodgers, former Cambridge Dodger Chris Van Cuyk is seen having fun with his wife and daughter.

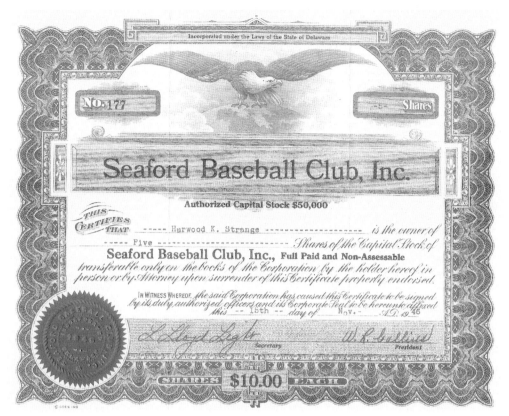

1946 SEAFORD EAGLES STOCK CERTIFICATE. Harwood Strange was a sportswriter for the local Seaford newspaper during the Eagles' four-year run. This Seaford Eagles stock certificate was issued to Strange in 1946 for five shares at $10 a share.

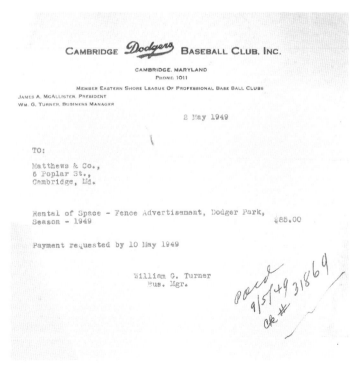

1949 CAMBRIDGE DODGERS LETTER. The letter at right, concerning the renting of billboard space at the Cambridge ballpark, provides a rare example of the Cambridge Dodgers letterhead.

THANK YOU!
SEAFORD
BASEBALL FANS!

Several weeks ago we told you that greater attendance at gates was necessary if the Seaford Baseball Club was to continue as a solvent organization. We "laid our cards on the table" and you understood our problem.

We are happy to report that attendance is very much improved, and with your continued help we shall end the season satisfactorily.

Won't you make a special effort to keep attending all games for the rest of the season?

Board of Directors
SEAFORD BASEBALL CLUB

SEAFORD EAGLES BASEBALL CLUB FAN MESSAGE. This message addressing the Seaford Eagles fans was printed in a local newspaper near the end of the 1949 season. As usual, attendance was the league's most pressing issue. The Eastern Shore League shut down for good soon after this message was printed.

BALL FOUR
PROMINENT PLAYERS

Throughout the entire existence of the Eastern Shore League, many players, homegrown and not, excited the scores of baseball fans on the Delmarva Peninsula. For a combined 15 years, the local faithful cheered their favorite teams and players, including many who had played, or would eventually play, in the major leagues. Four men who played in the ESHL even wound up in Cooperstown: Frank "Home Run" Baker, Jimmie Foxx, Red Ruffing, and Mickey Cochrane are all enshrined in the Baseball Hall of Fame. Many other stars and future major-league managers excelled during the ESHL's three eras; men such as Steve Bilko, Mickey Vernon, Paul Richards, Chris Van Cuyk, and Don Zimmer. Jack Sanford played for the Dover Phillies in 1948 and went on to win the 1957 National League Rookie of the Year award with the Philadelphia Phillies.

The Eastern Shore League's three eras were wonderful in that its fans were able to watch many fine ball players—some bound for the big leagues and some not—play the game the way it was meant to be played. It wasn't money that drove the players of yesterday; passion and love of the game motivated these men to play as hard as they possibly could, and this made for exciting times for Delmarva's baseball fans. This final chapter pays tribute to just a few of the many prominent baseball players who graced the ball fields in the ESHL's three magnificent eras.

DON ZIMMER, 1949 CAMBRIDGE DODGERS. Seen here in his Brooklyn Dodgers uniform, Don Zimmer began his professional baseball career at Cambridge in 1949. Zimmer played for five different teams in the majors, including the Chicago Cubs, where he was a National League All-Star in 1961. After completing 12 seasons in the majors, Zimmer managed four big-league teams and was named National League Manager of the Year in 1989 while piloting the Chicago Cubs. Don Zimmer currently is an advisor for the Tampa Bay Rays in the American League. (Courtesy of Brace Photo.)

HOME RUN BAKER, 1924 EASTON FARMERS. Baseball Hall of Famer Baker hailed from the town of Trappe on the Eastern Shore of Maryland. He was a star player for the Philadelphia A's from 1908 to 1914 and then the New York Yankees from 1916 to 1919 and again from 1921 to 1922. Baker sat out the 1915 season because of a contract dispute with the A's and retired in 1920 before returning to the Yankees in 1921. Frank Baker earned the nickname "Home Run" after he hit two crucial home runs to lead the A's to a World Series Championship in 1911. Although hitting only 96 career home runs, Baker led the American League in round trippers from 1911 to 1914 with 11, 10, 12, and 9 dingers respectively. (Courtesy of Brace Photo.)

PAUL RICHARDS, 1926 CRISFIELD CRABBERS. Shown in his Baltimore Orioles uniform, Paul Richards played for the Crisfield Crabbers in the ESHL in 1926 and 1927, hitting over .300 both years. Richards spent eight seasons in the big leagues, playing for four different teams from 1932 to 1946 and winning a world championship in 1945 with the Detroit Tigers. Richards went on to manage three teams in the majors, including the Baltimore Orioles from 1955 to 1961. While serving as the Orioles' general manager, Richards signed future Hall of Fame third-baseman Brooks Robinson. (Courtesy of Brace Photo.)

RED RUFFING, 1924 DOVER SENATORS. Charles "Red" Ruffing was called up to the Boston Red Sox from the Dover Senators at the age of 19. Some 22 years later, Ruffing finished his major-league career with 273 wins. A six-time All-Star, Ruffing was also a six-time world champion as a member of the New York Yankees, including the legendary 1927 Yankees, for which he led the league in strikeouts with 190. A great pitcher, Ruffing was also a pretty good hitter, ending his career with over 500 hits and slugging 36 major-league home runs. He was inducted into the National Baseball Hall of Fame in 1967. (Courtesy of Brace Photo.)

DANNY MURTAUGH, 1937 CAMBRIDGE CARDINALS. As a member of the EHSL's 1937 and 1938 Cambridge Cardinals, Danny Murtaugh enjoyed much success, hitting .297 and .312, respectively. Murtaugh went on to play for three teams in the National League during his nine-year major-league career. It was in his managerial career that Murtaugh gained his most success, however, winning world championships while managing the Pittsburgh Pirates in 1960 and 1971. He managed three different stints with the Pirates for a total of 15 years, ending his last reign in 1976. Murtaugh's No. 40 was retired by the Pittsburgh Pirates in 1977. (Courtesy of Brace Photo.)

JIMMIE FOXX, 1924 EASTON FARMERS. "Double X" is what they called Eastern Shore native Jimmie Foxx. He began his professional baseball career as a 16-year-old member of the ESHL's Easton Farmers. Foxx was a major-leaguer for 20 seasons, finishing with 534 home runs. An American League MVP on three occasions, Foxx won baseball's prestigious Triple Crown in 1933 with a batting average of .356 while slugging 48 home runs and driving in a whopping 163 runs. Foxx was a nine-time All-Star and was inducted into the National Baseball Hall of Fame in 1951. (Courtesy of Brace Photo.)

JOE MUIR, 1947 REHOBOTH BEACH PIRATES. In 1947, Eastern Shore native Joe Muir won 13 games for the Rehoboth Beach Pirates in the ESHL. Muir, born in the small town of Oriole, Maryland, went on to pitch for the Pittsburgh Pirates in the National League during the 1951 and 1952 seasons. His card is No. 154 in the Topps 1952 baseball card set, the first comprehensive baseball card set ever produced. Joe Muir is the uncle of Leroy Muir, to whom this book is dedicated. (Courtesy of Brace Photo.)

CARL FURILLO, 1940 POCOMOKE CITY CHICKS. Carl Furillo played for one year in the ESHL with the Pocomoke City Chicks, batting .319 for the 1940 season. Furillo went on to star for the Brooklyn and Los Angeles Dodgers for 15 years, leading the National League in 1953 with a .344 average. A two-time National League All-Star, Furillo won two world championships with the Dodgers, once with Brooklyn in 1955 and once with Los Angeles in 1959. After the Dodgers released him in 1960, Furillo felt ill-treated, and he sued them. He was awarded back pay by the courts, but he was unable to find a job anywhere in baseball. He left the sport, never to return, and worked several jobs before his death, including a stint installing elevators at the World Trade Center. (Courtesy of Brace Photo.)

SID GORDON, 1938 MILFORD GIANTS. During his one-year stay with the Milford Giants in the ESHL, Sid Gordon hit for a .352 average and slugged 25 home runs. The two-time National League All-Star played with three teams during his 13-year major-league career, finishing with over 200 major-league home runs. In 1975, while playing softball, the 57-year-old Gordon suffered a fatal heart attack. (Courtesy of Brace Photo.)

MICKEY VERNON, 1937 EASTON BROWNS. Mickey Vernon began his long and distinguished baseball career at Easton, Maryland, in the ESHL. In 20 major-league seasons with four teams (most of them with the Washington Senators), Vernon was named an American League All-Star seven times. While with the Senators, Vernon won the AL batting title in 1946 (.353) and 1953 (.337). After his fine playing career ended, Vernon managed the Washington Senators from 1961 to 1963. (Courtesy of Brace Photo.)

EASTERN SHORE LEAGUE

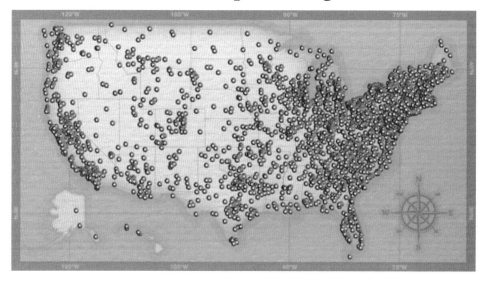